Finish What You Start

UNLOCKING THE SUCCESS SECRETS OF THE **TOP 1%**

Craig S. Copeland

FINISH WHAT YOU START. Copyright © 2010 by Craig S. Copeland. All rights reserved. Printed in the United States of America. No part of this book may be used or reproduced in any manner whatsoever without written permission except in the case of brief quotations embodied in critical articles and review. For information, address Reach Now Institute, Inc. 2935 South Sepulveda Blvd., Los Angeles, CA 90064

Visit our Web site at www.Finish-What-You-Start.com

Printed in the United States of America

First Printing: March 2010

Library of Congress Control Number: 2010903612

Publisher's Cataloging-in-Publication data

Copeland, Craig S.
    Finish what you start : Unlocking The Success Secrets Of The Top 1% / Craig S. Copeland.
        p. cm.
    ISBN 978-0-615-35906-9
    1. Success. 2. Success in business. 3. Self Improvement
    4. Self-actualization (Psychology). 5. Self-help techniques.
    I. Finish what you start : Unlocking The Success Secrets Of The Top 1%.
    II. Title.

BF637.S4 .C665 2010
158.1—dc22

                                                              2010903612

Praise for
Finish What You Start

"Fast, effective, simple to digest.
If you don't reach your goals, you didn't read the book."

— **Jack Canfield**, Co-author of *The Success Principles* and
Co-creator of the *Chicken Soup for the Soul* series

"Craig's book and program gives you five fast, effective strategies
to succeed at a higher level than ever before."

— **Brian Tracy**, author of *Maximum Achievement*

"Craig Copeland gets it - you can't succeed alone.
Finish What You Start leverages the success strategies of the
world's top performers so that you can achieve your goals."

— **Keith Ferrazzi**, author of NY Times #1 Bestseller of
Who's Got Your Back and *Never Eat Alone*

"This book contains a simple idea that is critically important
if you want to create long-term success in your life. If you
implement only *"Power Principle #1"* from this book in your life,
that alone will dramatically increase your success."

— **Eben Pagan**, Creator of *GetAltitude* and *Wake Up Productive*

"Craig's book and training has great insight,
and merits attention."

— **Nathaniel Branden Ph.D.**, author of *My Years with Ayn Rand*

Acknowledgements

To say that these people were helpful in the creation of this book would be an understatement.

To my new mentor, Brian Tracy who's suggestion of a slightly new direction changed everything for the better. To Jack Canfield whose mentorship, advice, and generosity are the very spirit of this book. Thanks to Eben Pagan who is not only a great mentor but a very generous individual who gave me my start. Thanks also to Keith Ferrazzi who has been a great guide and has offered nothing but encouragement and tons of yes(es). Thanks to Tim Ferriss, one of the smartest people I know; yes, I will crush it! Thank you to Joseph McClendon III whose energy and enthusiasm have become the foundation for which I too strive to always better myself. To Eric Delabarre whose coaching and mentoring brought this book to life before my very eyes. To Renese Howell for kindly and gently resolving my grammatical faux pas(s) with tact and diplomacy. To Erin McGonigle for her support, editing, and sisterly love. To Jerri Palumbo whose encouragement, animalistic business savvy, dedication, and support are the reasons this book is even here today. To Shari Macdonald whose love, support, and clarity are the very foundations of what's inside these pages. To Zoe Quist for using these very principles to reach her own goals and pursuits thru long hours of bonding, pain, laughter, and talent. To David Rogers for his support and Rain-Man-like knowledge about this industry. To Barry Swerdlick who provided encouragement and great insights. To Sue Black who helped the vision of my book become reality. To Jennifer Mola, a smart and savvy friend who embodies these *Power Principles* in everything she does. To Wanda Snell whose support and kindness lifts me in many ways. And of course to Nancy Larrew who has always encouraged me in every endeavor and even showed her trust through investing the first few dollars that gave me my start.

To my mother, Arlene Copeland, who was more of an angel than even I realized.

To my dog, North who by virtue of a wag and happy smile made me a better person than I knew I could be.

Success can be achieved by anyone.

Anyone who has a dream can have success. You don't need money, talent, education, or family connections to be successful, just perseverance. Find your passion and the money will follow. You don't even need to possess a special talent or education, only the drive and the willingness to learn. When you're open to growing and gaining knowledge you become increasingly more powerful and confident. Success is not gained through family connections; it's accomplished by making a decision, then taking action toward your goals. The only one who can make you successful is you. Once you become aware of this, you begin to create a world others want to be a part of.

I wrote this book because there is no one in the world who can't reach their goals, fulfill their dreams, or finish what they start. All you have to do is make a decision to begin today...

Contents

Part 1 - Creating Unstoppable Success

Part 2 - Building A New Foundation

Part 3 - Creating Success That Sticks

Preface

This book was written and designed to give you the tools to accomplish your goals by showing you what successful people do. It's funny but a large percentage of people are already aware of these tools, however, they don't use them. In fact, many already know how to set goals. Good goals. Worthy goals. Yet few know how to actually reach them. As smart as they are—and they are smart—driven, ambitious, or determined to once and for all reach their goals, few reach them. Somewhere along the way they get derailed and lose sight of their objective only to find that it's now five or ten years later and that incredible, once in a lifetime goal is collecting dust on the shelf.

I'm going to show you the tools you need to reach your goals and how to use them in ways that benefit you most, and I'll also show you how easy they are to use. We're going to be examining those few who are the most successful, how they got there, and what keeps them constantly rising to the top. Best of all, we'll walk through the tools they use so you too can start using them to get to the level of success you desire in your life. You should have the same rewards of success, and it's within your power to achieve them.

Whether you're starting at the bottom rung of the ladder, or you're already enjoying success that others envy, this book contains universal principles successful people everywhere have always used to achieve the kind of results they desire in life. Whether your goals are in the areas of your career, your finances, your fitness and health, your relationships, or a combination of the above, you simply need the proper tools and direction to help you get to the next level. You won't find any "tricks" for getting there within this book. There's no magic elixir or secret words you'll need to know. But there is a formula for success, and it's simple to learn. And, you'll need to know it in order to become successful. I discovered this formula by accident while working with and observing some of the world's most successful people, because I also wanted to achieve the same kinds of successes they enjoy. I've distilled this formula into what I call the 5 *Power Principles*.

I myself struggled for many years. I grew up in a household that had only one bed. Yet I always knew there was something better out there for me, I just didn't know what it was or how I would get there. It wasn't until years later that I discovered an entryway to the tools that would teach me how to be successful.

Prior to the work I do now, I was a top Personal Assistant to CEOs and high-level Executives, Grammy-winning artists, Producers, Entrepreneurs, A-list Actors and others for about fifteen years. Some of the people I've worked with are household names, while others are more obscure, but equally renowned in their fields. After years of struggling with my goals and objectives for my own life and success, I have discovered that all of them had learned how to obtain the ability to achieve the success that they desired, and I was determined to discover that same formula for myself.

In my position as a Personal Assistant, I had the opportunity to become a fly on the wall when in their presence. It was like being given a backstage pass to an exclusive VIP event. Observing them over many years, I noticed something that flipped my entire world upside down.

Each one of these highly successful people had several friends and associates they met with in person or spoke on the phone with on a regular basis. And every time they'd walk away from the encounter, they became even more empowered, energetic, and mission-driven than ever before. It was like they got a B12 shot right there and now they were revved up to handle even greater challenges.

So, like a ninja, staying in the background, learning and observing, I listened, absorbed and discovered the formula that gave them their power to become the incredibly successful people they are today.

When talking to their friends or associates they'd share where they presently were with a particular project, client, or goal. Then the other person would offer their experience, feedback, praise, acknowledgment, services, and guidance to carry them even further.

By the time they ended their conversation, my boss(es) would go into a whole other gear and became UNSTOPPABLE.

After just one or two conversations, he would become like Seabiscuit, leaving his competition in the dust.

It was amazing to watch and this phenomenon kept happening again and again.

I saw the same results in ALL my bosses. It was like a coda that they all had access to and the rest of us didn't.

This was so incredibly simple yet so POWERFUL.

What was going on here? I wasn't quite sure what I was seeing so I had to break this down to truly understand.

I began to ask questions, and while they weren't always cognizant of everything they themselves did to create a formula for their success, I was soon given some unique insights into what each of them did and how they did it to achieve their personal levels of success. While all of them were distinctly different people, from various walks of life, and with entirely different personal objectives, looking at their habits and behaviors from an outside perspective, I began to see a common thread each of them shared.

Some had failed along the way and had to pick up and start over again. But this rarely kept them down for very long and in fact most hardly missed a beat. For them, understanding what wasn't working and then readjusting their methods was like a burst of adrenalin.

And, it was much more than what many refer to as a Mastermind group, as coined by Napoleon Hill. They surrounded themselves with like-minded people and used the power of these other people to accelerate their own goals. They also incorporated additional tools and techniques that became part of the formula necessary to obtain their personal successes. I noticed the pattern rarely ever changed. What I also noticed is that the energy dynamic of these groups was an important component to their success. When some could not participate in a consistent fashion, that dynamic changed. It was here that I first began to create a method whereby this would no longer become a disadvantage. A method that I'm going to teach you.

In creating the 5 *Power Principles*, I took the key elements that became the formula (coda) for success. Through hours of personal trial and error, and using other people to further test my theories to help hone my methods, I've developed a system that is consistently proving both sound and accurate. In fact, in speaking to other successful entrepreneurs about these *Power Principles* and their repeated effectiveness, time and time again I get the same resounding feedback that I've struck onto something most profound. In turn, they too are excited to use the practices and techniques I've developed.

Is reading this book all you need to become successful? Well, no. Sitting on the sidelines and reading a book on improvement or motivation will not do the trick. You're going to need to get up and get active. You're going to have to do the exercises and practice the behaviors outlined in this book. But one of the key differences between my *Power Principles* and methods taught by others for success is that the *Power Principles* will work for anyone at any level of success; it doesn't matter if you're new or already well on your way to creating success in your life now. The steps are not hard to practice. In fact, you'll find you will only need a very small portion of your day to practice them effectively. While the exercises may seem uncomfortable when you first begin to practice them - like any new endeavor you take on - I've found that people see great value in the principles, and as they continue to practice them, they commit even more to sticking with them to the end. In time they get easier and more fun to absorb!

How much time will it take to practice these principles? You may find you'll only need as much time as you do for a simple phone call, or the time it takes to listen to a couple songs on the radio. To achieve even greater results, of course, you will want to put more time into practicing the *Power Principles*. It's entirely up to you how much energy and focus you choose to dedicate to seeing the results you want. It's the difference between becoming a competent snow boarder and becoming a great one. As with everything in life, the more time, effort, and focus you devote, the greater the reward.

How you spend your time applying the *Power Principles* is also up to you. If you've ever needed to straighten up your home you knew you could do it all at once or you could spread it out over several days. The same concept applies when you're practicing the exercises throughout this book. It's all up to you. And as you improve in your application of the 5 *Power Principles*, you'll notice that it will take you less and less time each day to *straighten your own house.*

If you're like most people, you'll find that you're already using some or all of these principles in your daily life on some level. As you'll learn throughout this book, you're just not using them together as a complete formula yet. And once you do, you'll see that these principles are so fundamental to how we were designed as human beings to live and interact with other human beings for even greater levels of success.

One of the guiding principles behind this book is to take the "self" out of self-help. While that may seem counter intuitive to you at first, it's my expectation that it will begin to make perfect sense to you as you read this book and practice the exercises. The 5 *Power Principles* are the key. They're a complete set of simple, empowering tools that you can begin to master in practically no time at all. Using them together will enable you to succeed in any goal.

One thing that keeps people from completing what they start is when "life gets in the way." There may also be times when you'll hear a voice inside you saying you don't really need to do the exercises. Don't listen. The things that get in the way are almost always things that come up in life time and time again giving us an excuse to stray from our chosen path. You've probably already experienced how major and minor challenges in your life can trip you up, pull you off your course, make you feel sad, tired, overworked, or stressed. And there are at least a hundred more "great" excuses that can keep us from finishing what we've started. I'm going to show you how these "excuses" can become things of the past that never bother you again.

I'm here to tell you that while it's not completely your fault, you do have to take some ownership here and do the exercises. You'll find that these 5 *Power Principles* are amazingly easy to do. Unlike most other programs you've tried, as you continue to apply the 5 *Power Principles* you'll find they will quickly and naturally become a part of your regular routine, and become easier for you to master. You'll rapidly begin seeing results, and you'll soon forget you're even doing the exercises!

Looking at this book's Table of Contents, you may wonder why I don't give you all 5 of the *Power Principles* early on in the book? That's because I want to set you up with the concepts you'll need to apply the 5 *Power Principles* effectively in your life. Like Mr. Miyagi in *The Karate Kid* (wax on, wax off). I want to guide you so you'll see how the 5 *Power Principles* will work before you start to consciously apply them. By the time you get to the section where I explain each one in greater detail, you'll already have a better understanding of their benefits for you. I also want you to see and experience how easy the principles are going to be to use in your life, so I'll introduce the first Power Principle earlier than the others. It's the most basic, fundamental, and easiest to understand of the 5 *Power Principles*, and successfully mastering it will help you have even greater success with all the others. Each of the *Power Principles* are simple to grasp, and there are only five in total. That's it!

This book is laid out so as you read it and do the exercises, you'll gain knowledge and understanding of the 5 *Power Principles* immediately and an awareness of how they can work for you. Each of them can be incorporated seamlessly into your life.

I'm not a doctor. I'm not a professor, scientist, or certified authority.

What I am is someone who has had the good fortune, opportunity and experience to indoctrinate myself into the world of the top one percent and was blessed with over fifteen years of observation, recognizing the commonalities of their individual successes, and those of their families and associates. I've distilled from countless hours of observation, in depth interviews, and reaffirmation of these principles and practices, the tools necessary for repeated successes in reaching one's personal goals and business objectives. Now, I too enjoy the success benefits these *5 Power Principles* offer for my own life and personal goals.

As you master these principles, you'll also see that you will experience much more energy and drive, and it will be easier to go after whatever you desire and finally *finish what you start.* The increased momentum you experience as you complete more and more of your tasks and goals will also give you a surge of inner power, and you'll find you're on a path of unstoppable success.

How this book works to get you to the finish line:

This book is specifically broken into sections and each one has a very specific purpose.

Section One: Is set up to give you the framework and understanding of the *Finish What You Start* system through examples and instructions.

Section Two: Starts you on your journey towards creating new habits and behaviors within yourself. These habits will begin to change your thinking process and open your awareness to quickly and correctly choose the right path towards your goal.

Section Three: Gives you the *Power Principles* already laid out in a way so you can see what you're doing, the proper way to do it, and the best method in which to do it. This section spells out what to do and what to look for.

Section Four: Wraps it all up by giving you a few more tools and some road markers to help you stay on track. By the time you get to this section your goal reaching habits should now come to you more quickly and be easier for you to handle. By this time you will have reached the finish line for both small and large tasks.

Are you ready to get started on this path? Let's go!

Introduction:

What's the first important thing they always tell you to do on an airplane? OK, after they show you how to fasten your seatbelt. It's to put your own oxygen mask on first before helping someone else with theirs. Why? The answer is simple: *You can't help others before you help yourself.*

I'd like you to keep this concept in mind as you read through this book. As your mind shifts towards the process of *finishing what you start*, you're going to need this mindset to help you envision reaching your goals. This one simple instruction may seem selfish on the surface, but you'll find that it becomes one of the most selfless acts you'll ever learn. And if you apply this same principle toward your own life, you'll begin to truly see the world in an entirely different way. And, for perhaps the first time in your life, you'll start to understand that what you may have viewed as a selfish idea in the past, turned out to be a concept that empowers you to accomplish greater things, and thereby help others to do the same.

By taking care of yourself first, you create a framework for your life that is unstoppable. And once your successes begin to build up and multiply, you'll see how much easier it is for you to help others. Suddenly people will begin seeking you out for advice. No longer will your objectives, goals, and tasks seem at all overwhelming or out-of-reach. You'll quickly become a master at *creating unstoppable success* once and for all.

Like any alchemic formula, the *Power Principles* are not new. They're not revolutionary. However the power of alchemy is potent, even explosive. Take something as simple as gunpowder, which consists of saltpeter (potassium nitrate), charcoal (for carbon), and sulfur. By themselves, all of these ingredients are significant, but basically harmless. However, when mixed together, they create a powerful force to be reckoned with. Or take simple pig iron. When you combine it with carbon, silicon, manganese, sulfur, and phosphorus, in the right proportions, you create the strongest of steel. This same law applies to the 5 *Power Principles*. Each one by itself is strong and self-sustaining, and has been around practically forever. But when used together in the right way, the 5 *Power Principles* create a potent formula of dynamic energy whose recipe always spells V-I-C-T-O-R-Y. Your goal will be learning to use them in the right combination to achieve your ultimate success.

Self-help has transformed into an explosive phenomenon for more than 20 years now.

In the early 1970s, if you walked into most bookstores you'd be hard pressed to find but a handful of books on self-help. I personally can remember some of my early favorites by authors like Dr. Wayne Dyer, Barbara De Angelis, Dale Carnegie, M. Scott Peck, and Normal Vincent Peale, just to name a few.

Just how explosive has the growth of self-help become? Today, if you go into any bookstore you'll find row after row of books on self-improvement and motivation by authors like Stephen Covey, Tony Robbins, Brian Tracy, Jim Rohn, Mark Victor Hansen, T. Harv Eker, John C, Maxwell, Jack Canfield and others. Self-help and Self-Improvement is now close to a $13 billion dollar industry. So what's changed? And, more importantly, with all these books available to us, why does it seem we aren't getting any better? If we go by the amount of books we have out there, on the surface, it looks like perhaps we're getting worse.

Part of the reason why this section of the bookstore keeps expanding is because a number of authors have gone from writing self-help books to becoming motivational and self-improvement authors. Some stores have even got a little marketing savvy and started putting these books closer to the fitness and weight loss sections. But if you look beneath the surface, it's because more and more people are feeling left out, left behind, or alone. Somehow, between the 1980s to the 2000s, more and more people have begun looking for answers as to why their lives seem so empty.

You can confirm this by doing a Google search on the number of 12-Step programs that have popped up over the years. In the beginning there were only four basic programs: Alcoholics Anonymous, Cocaine Anonymous, Al-Anon (for friends and families of Alcoholics), and Alateen for teenagers who are struggling with the problems of addiction or have family members or friends who are substance abusers. But nowadays, there are over *two-hundred* types of 12-Step programs! They're set up to help over-eaters, workaholics, gamblers, co-dependents, debtors, narcotics abusers, clutter addicts, technology dependence, and people who are hooked on pills or sex to help them cope with life.

So why haven't we gotten any better? Why are more people feeling lost, in need, lonely, confused, and looking for help? And why are there so many self-acknowledged gurus out there who profess to have the answers or cure for all of our ills, when they're really just offering us another band-aid?

To truly understand self-help you have to look at its purpose. According to Webster's Dictionary, self-help is: *the action or process of bettering oneself or overcoming one's problems without the aid of others;*

especially: the coping with one's personal or emotional problems without professional help.

Self-help is supposed to help us become better people, to improve ourselves, and give us the tools to increase to our full potential and achieve success. Everyone strives to make their lives better, and to improve their living environment. This can include things like remodeling our kitchens, buying a nice plasma TV for the living room, investing in a front-loading washer and dryer, and nice, plush furniture. By improving our homes - the place where we live and spend most of our time - we feel better about ourselves, more confident, happier, and more successful - at least for a while.

And when we're not trying to improve our environment, we're trying to fix ourselves. We're taking steps to lose weight, or going to the gym to get into shape. We take courses to improve our status in life - courses to help us invest, to get rich, to get a better job, or to become our own boss. If we're single, we strive to find the love of our lives: our soul mate, the one who we think is going to complete us and make us whole. There are even courses to help us improve how we feel about ourselves so we're more capable and successful. We invest our money and time on courses to help us become a better speaker, entrepreneur, leader, and human being.

So in principle, self-help is a good thing. It's fundamentally there to increase and improve our lives. And who doesn't want a better life? Why settle for less? If the tools are out there to make us better, more successful, more amazing human beings, shouldn't we do everything we can to get there? And the authors of self-help books, seminars, CDs, DVDs, and classes all do their best to help us become the best person we can be.

So why is it that most people drop out of self-help programs after only a couple weeks or a few months, only to end up taking another course down the road? Are we just sold a different bill of goods over and over to keep us hooked? This question drove me more than anything else to find the answers.

And why do we need to go to an outside source to learn these things? After all, there are many competent, successful people who have never taken a self-help course. How did they acquire these skills? Were they born with them?

It was recently suggested by one multi-million dollar seminar company based in San Francisco that the reason people take additional seminars is because after a while of working on their goals alone, they miss the camaraderie and companionship they found in the seminars and workshops, which require group participation. This group energy provides added comforts to them, and helps to sustain them. In the world of self improvement, it seems that the vast majority of people - some seasoned speaking professionals say at least eighty percent - who take some form of self improvement course end up dropping out or failing, while about ten to twenty percent seem to improve and go on to have successful lives. This off-balance statistic seems to also hold true in the entrepreneurial world as well.

This is not to discredit self improvement, or to make you feel bad for wanting to improve yourself. In fact, by giving you the proper foundations of learning and support behind you, this book will make any self-help or self-improvement program you decide to use even more effective by helping you finish what you start. My purpose in highlighting some of the fundamental problems with the self-help community is to point you in the right direction so that when you do take on any kind of improvement course in the future, you'll succeed and not drop out, fail, or give up. I want you to be able to complete and carry through any goal you set your mind to. Won't it be great when the lessons you learn in any course for self-improvement actually stick with you?

You may have found yourself feeling resentful after taking self-improvement courses to find yourself later on spending even more money on yet another book, or finding that you have to take additional courses because you didn't finish what you started. You felt frustrated, and still you keep on trying again and again, hoping that this time the program will work for you! You were finally going to lose that weight, land that great job, meet the person of your dreams, and have the riches you truly desire.

We, as a society, keep on buying more and more products to improve our lives, thinking that this latest product or course will be the one. And while a number of these self-help products actually do as promised, a large number of us do not complete them. So why do we keep buying these things? Why do we go to the bookstore to get one more book that will hopefully fix everything this time?

I know what that's like. I've done this myself! When I was younger, I read more books on self-help and self-improvement than most people. And most of those books ended up as legs for a table that I put together with a piece of plywood for the tabletop.

Every new book that came along and had a compelling title was another one that I had to own. I couldn't take the chance… this time this was going to be the one that provided all the answers.

I practically grew up on self-help because, like a lot of people, I'd always felt like I was less than everyone else. It was as if I wasn't clued in because I somehow didn't get the secret manual for life that everyone else got. So I read every book I could get my hands on that promised to make me a better, greater, happier, more successful, richer, stronger, fitter, better speaking, more attractive, smarter, funnier, person. Then when the authors wrote another book I'd buy that one too. Why? Why wasn't the first one or two enough? What was it that I wasn't getting? Was I not as smart as others? Sure the lessons stuck with me for a while, but after some time passed I began to notice I was feeling those old feelings of low self-worth again. Old behaviors were resurfacing. What was going on?

When I was younger, I was told by a not-too-favorite relative that I'd scored very low on a school IQ test. The way it was put to me, I scored lower than every other student. Now that might not seem like much but I was eleven. And at the age of eleven, fitting in means everything to a child. At the time I didn't understand this was their way of keeping me down and in their control. It wouldn't be until many years later that I'd learn in fact that was never the case.

But it must have been true because I also equated being poor with being stupid. In the household I grew up in we only had one bed until I was around 15 years old. My mother slept in the living room until we were forced out by rat infestations. I remember always feeling embarrassed and ashamed to have friends over.

And because my mother had to work all the time to support us, I was left alone a lot. They called it being a latch-key kid. So I always looked for the simplest path to take and the one I'd have to put the least amount of work and effort into. To fit in I became the class clown. It helped me to feel like I was part of the group. To distance myself from becoming close to others I ditched school as much as I could get away with. Because I never wanted to get too close and have people find out I was poor and not like them. I stole money or whatever else I could get away with, and chose to play more than I studied. And while I thought this was the easiest path to get through life, it turned out to be the hardest. If I had the hindsight I did many years later, I would have learned that it took me more time, much more effort, a lot more money, and great personal struggle to learn how to undo every backwards thing I set in place for myself rather than to just acquire the disciplines of learning how to do it better, smarter, and ultimately faster than I (wrongly) thought – at the time – I was doing.

I always thought I was always being so clever and out-foxing everyone I met, that at one point in my life when I was attending the Al-anon program (for friends and family of alcoholics) for several years, I used to have a slight-of-hand technique I was taught on the streets where I'd pretend to put a twenty dollar bill into the basket they passed around to help defer costs and pay for coffee, cookies, and the room. But instead of actually putting in twenty dollars, using slight of hand, I really only put in a one dollar bill but I still made change of nineteen dollars which I took for myself at every meeting I attended. In other words, I was taking nineteen dollars from them in exchange for my one dollar. They were losing eighteen dollars every time I got hold of the basket. This went on for three years.

Then it happened. The day that would alter my life. After thinking I'd been so clever all of those years, fooling all of those suckers, one day after being in the program for three years, I was asked to speak in front of the room of people for twenty minutes. At the time I could not fathom why they chose me. I wasn't sure what I was going to even talk about. But when I began things suddenly just started to pour out of me like a dam had burst. For the first time I was feeling this great pressure being released from within me. And I cried. Then cried some more. Where the heck was all this coming from?

It was during this cathartic talk that I found myself confessing what I had been doing in those meeting rooms all those years. I told them about the money I'd been stealing. In fact, I blurted it out, almost yelling, what I'd done, that I was wrong, and that I was so sorry. And I cried some more.

I thought right then and there that they'd lynch me. And instead of getting carried out of there on a rail and being tarred and feathered, they laughed out loud when I admitted this petty crime. What was going on? Why weren't people picking up stones and throwing them at me? Then someone shouted out from the back of the room; "We know, you idiot. We've known about it for years. Why do you think we kept asking you to come back?" That only ensued a bigger roar of laughter.

It was in that moment that I realized I hadn't been fooling anyone. It wasn't that I'd been testing their intentions towards me all those years, like I'd thought. I'd been testing my own intentions, and I had failed miserably! I'd let every one of them down. But that's not how they saw it at all. They saw someone who had been in so much pain and discomfort that they knew I needed those rooms more than ever. And that I needed the love and the support they couldn't force upon me, only to be there for me when I needed them and let me find it on my own.

Afterwards they came up one by one and hugged me. I hadn't fooled anyone but myself and yet they still loved, encouraged, and supported me. They saw me as a better person then I had ever seen in myself. And in that instant everything changed for me.

My world was different. I felt like I could trust myself again. I began to put in more hours serving and supporting the people in those meetings. I made it my mission to put in more hours than anyone else.

Soon I started doing volunteer work outside of the meetings as well and serving food in soup kitchens downtown and in the soup lines in Santa Monica. Under the guidance of others I started to go to the library and read to children. I drove to poor neighborhoods and handed out clothing to needy families. I started not just to give back, but give beyond what I had ever given before because I was filled with such lightheartedness and energy.

That room of people who I thought were all fools, turned out to be my teachers, my family, my mentors, and my inspiration. And they taught me the power of getting out of my own way.

I began to realize how it all starts with children. That if we reach them at an early stage in their lives they won't have to struggle later in life as I did to learn what others learned about how life and community can work for you, not against you. If given the opportunity, people want to help and guide you if you let them.

It's because I had learned to open myself up like this and be given a new opportunity and a better outlook on life that I began working hard on improving myself. I started reading all the books I'd skipped in school. I asked everyone questions. I became very curious about things in life. And through a series of trial and error jobs I held, after many years of hard work and focus, I found a calling and made a career as a successful Personal Assistant for over fifteen years. And it's through that journey that I became a better part of the world, my community, and I became someone who was more receptive to the lessons and success principles I ended up learning and then one day teaching; the lessons I'd learned from the top successful people I had the privilege to work for.

Oh, by the way, I read one to four books a week and still can't get enough. I still do volunteer work now more than ever. I became a crisis intervention counselor, and I am a guy who loves talking to and meeting all kinds of people.

It was through this gift I was given, that I got an even bigger gift. The gift of the success *Power Principles* that are the foundation of my book and my teachings. Had I not gone through that journey of shedding my old skin of bad behaviors, I never, in a millions years, would have ended up in a place where the top people in their industries would ever even think of hiring me.

And like we all do in our journey and struggle to become someone great, I wanted to become someone who can offer something back to the very world that we all strive to be successful in.

Because of the lessons I ultimately learned from working with the top one percent, I now have the opportunity to share what I've learned with you, and give you the same gifts of insights and tools that can benefit you and allow you the opportunity to become successful in your own life to reach your biggest dreams, finish what you start, and share your own success with everyone you too will encounter.

It's true that as we grow and develop mentally we want to absorb more knowledge and information to help us keep improving ourselves and climbing the ladder. It's equally true that you can't go to the gym just once or twice, work out, get into great shape, and never have to go again. The same principle applies for losing weight or even taking courses in school. You need to keep up some type of maintenance program to retain the fundamentals of what you've learned and gain.

With so many books and courses on so many areas of improvement - relationships, wealth, success, happiness, health, and more - it seems that all of them lack one fundamental step that could finally help you stick with them, use their concepts, and complete them once and for all. In fact, so many self-help gurus have touched upon, danced around, and gotten *very* close to addressing the reason a majority of us don't complete our mission. The problem? It has to do with the way we as humans were designed to operate in the world.

It's in the word "self." We've become trained to improve ourselves all by ourselves. But that goes against our fundamental nature of being a valuable, contributing, loved, part of society.

The mission of this book is to answer and address those nagging questions as to why so few succeed and how to get you to succeed and reach your goals. Of course, these *Power Principles* were created out of observing common threads of habits and behaviors that successful people use time and again to achieve their desired outcome. And for that reason alone, people who already are achieving huge successes in their own lives now can still incorporate these tools for creating their own levels of even greater accomplishment. And, continue climbing the ladder even higher, if you will.

Lastly, even though this book does address taking the *self* out of self-help, you'll instantly see how using the *Power Principles* actually strengthens and will exponentially improve the *self* to become more driven, more creative, more focused, and more successful.

Let's get right into it!

— *Framework* —

The tools of the *5 Power Principles* using the Foundation of CORE

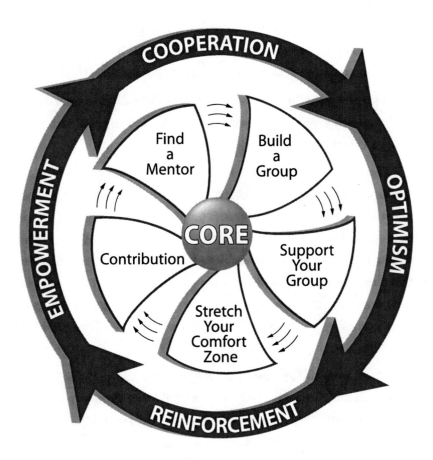

Part 1 —
Creating Unstoppable
Success

No Excuses

"Be the change you want to see in the world."

   - Mahatma Gandhi

One of my mentors, Brian Tracy, has said in his book "Goals!" that he has found over and over again how a person of average intelligence with clear goals will run circles around a genius who is not sure of what he or she really wants.

And a very wise friend of mine said that you *betray* yourself when you don't fully go after your biggest dreams and goals with every ounce of your passion and energy.

Why is it so important to go after your goals and reach them? No one wants to be rescued. Even people in trouble don't want to be rescued. Take the people of Katrina. Did they need rescuing? Yes. Did they want to have to be in a position where they needed to be rescued? No.

If given the choice, most want to be capable people who are a strong, valued part of society, and given the opportunity and the means, they often want to become someone who can also contribute to society. And all of them want to be successful, financially independent, happy, and loved.

So you are always given two choices. One is to decide that you are a victim. That life will never be easy, and what's the point in trying if you always end up struggling and inevitably in failure.

If we truly live in a world where we can manifest our own outcome, then this type of person will indeed become a great manifester of his own destiny. His destiny to fail will become his every time.

If instead you wish to become someone who finishes what you start and reach your success goals, then you too have a choice to make. Your path is always filled with adventure.

Think about this. The road ahead of you is filled with opportunities. You will always be the captain and it's you who decides which road you travel on. Sometimes the road will be hard and the path long. Sometimes you will meet friends and allies on the road. Other times you'll encounter those who are not always helpful to you. But it is always up to you where you go next.

As you travel down this road, you can ask directions. Those you meet along the way will know where to point you, some will not. You are an explorer creating new pathways of destiny and opportunity.

It has been said many times that people handed wealth will have a hard time keeping it. People who earn their wealth know how to gather it to them and maintain it.

As an explorer, you get to determine how fast or slow you travel. Who you'll befriend along the way. What tools you will need on your journey.

You may encounter someone who has traveled this same road and can give you insights to the shortcuts and pitfalls. The scenic portions of the roads and those filled only with shade. Use their counsel to make your journey enjoyable and the outcome even more successful for you.

Again, you are someone who manifests your destiny. If you choose to remain open to opportunities you will be rewarded with benefits along the way. But you also do not want to travel down this road blindly or unprepared.

When starting on any journey, you want to make sure you have the proper supplies and enough of them to last you on your trek. Sometimes you will not know how much you will need or exactly what you will need to get there. Here's a tip: A powerful tool of any explorer is to *ask*.

Ask as much as you can of those who've traveled this road before you. **Ask** those along the way. **Ask** if some would travel with you. And **ask** the friends you meet along the way how they think you are doing. *Asking* is the one thing people should do more, and yet most are afraid to do it at all.

Only you will know the outcome you're seeking and the end you wish to see when you arrive. It's through constant forward movement, keeping your eyes on your goal, and by taking action, that you will successfully reach your finish line.

The first thing you'll want to have in your arsenal is a passion or desire to reach your goals. You won't necessarily know how you're going to get there just yet, but you'll need to have the passion, ambition, and determination to achieve your desired outcome. It's said that the footwork is your responsibility; the results are up to God. That means two things: First, you cannot sit there and pray for the desired outcome and hope that God (or the universe, or whoever you pray to) will grant your desires. Even the book and video *The Secret* says that manifesting is not just about envisioning what you want, but in taking action towards getting it. And secondly, you must have a passion or deep desire to reach that goal. If you're lukewarm in your desires, they will never become a reality for you.

There are several types of people who go after a goal and fail. It's good to examine who these people are so you can avoid falling into their same traps of failure. By the way, all these people have the power within them to change their habits and achieve the success they desire. This means that if you recognize yourself in one or more of these personality types, you can start to make changes that will lead to your success. Let's take a look at these personality types now.

One such person who fails is *The Dreamer*. That person, who has the greatest of ideas and dreams yet takes no action to make them a reality. We all know someone like that. Perhaps it's even you. They have amazing, incredible, fresh ideas for a new TV show, or an innovative invention, or a new business venture, or an innovation that could become the next Google or iPhone. Yet, several years later, they're still talking about their "great" ideas and they haven't taken one step towards making them a reality. Why?

There are a number of reasons behind this. While their ideas may be great, they have no clue where to begin towards bringing their ideas into reality. So these ideas stay locked inside their minds, and ultimately become nothing more than a really good story to tell their friends at a dinner party. It's possible they did try to get something going, but ran into too many roadblocks early on and became frustrated, or have already wasted too much money. Or they may have been afraid to let anyone else know about their idea for fear of having it stolen. We've all known someone like this, someone who secretly wrote the next number one hit song, or they have a plan to end world hunger or a great idea to put anyone in need into a house on less than $10K a year, or the next great Coca-Cola. As we delve deeper into what it takes to become successful, we'll explore ways to unlock this personality type even more to help make their dreams and ideas become reality.

Then there's *The Procrastinator*. Those who have a genius idea, but get too bogged down with work or family obligations and decide they'll get to it later. Ten years later, they're still waiting for just the perfect time they need to get started and turn this idea into a reality.

Procrastination can come out of fear. We'll address how to recognize and manage these fears and how to work more effectively to push through them and create more productive results.

No one wants to procrastinate but few know how to kick-start their goals. Once you learn the techniques of this program you will have no trouble jumping in and taking immediate action. This will become pleasurable and something you always look forward to.

Then there are also those people who don't know how to become their own boss; known as *The Follower*. It's too overwhelming for them to figure out how to begin their project and so it never ever gets started. I myself used to fit into this category. I had worked for so many years for someone else that I couldn't even fathom how to do something where I was the lead on the project or needed to work entirely on my own.

The Follower never has to rely on himself. All he has to do is show up and do the tasks assigned to him. So when he does venture out on his own he does not know where to begin, how to start, or what tools he needs to be successful. He is so used to waiting for someone else to direct him that the confidence-muscles he needs for going after his own goals are weak. I'll show you how to re-develop these muscles that were not lost, just unused, make them stronger, more powerful, and how they can work to benefit you, not work against you.

If this personality type has been a problem for you, don't worry. Soon it will be a thing of the past.

Of course, there are many more different types of people who offer a variety of different excuses as to why they never accomplish their goals. The problem with all of their excuses is that they're exactly that - excuses. In today's world, no one can honestly say that having a lack of intelligence, money, power, important contacts, or family influence is what held them back. There are copious examples of people who have overcome some or all of these things. Instead, for the people who have succumbed to the failure personality types, it was their mind-set and their ability (or lack thereof) to take the first step... action.

To be successful at anything, you first need to make a decision that it is something you really want to become a reality. You decide that you're so passionate about it that you can't help but take immediate action. Then you need to take even more action. Remember about alchemy? For your dreams to become a reality, you will need to have a combination of one part imagination, one part desire or passion, one part decision, and one part action.

—— FINISH LINE EXERCISE ——

Are you someone who gets the JOB done or are you someone who lacks the ability to complete your task? Everyone wants to reach their goal. But we also know that life can get in the way making it harder to get there.

▶ What Type are you?:

1.   The Dreamer

2.   The Procrastinator

3.   The Follower

4.   Other _____

1. What ideas or inventions have you created that never got

    completed? ▶ *Write for 10 minutes on what great ideas or goals*

    you have sitting inside your head or hiding in a drawer gathering

    dust. (Remember, no one is checking your answers. Now is the

    time to be honest and open with yourself. Challenge yourself as

    you've never done before.)

—— FINISH LINE EXERCISE *continued* ——

2. What is holding you back? Is it being overwhelmed? Is it fear? Are you having time management issues? ▶ *Write for 5 minutes on what you feel may be keeping you from getting started and staying on track.*

3. What tools or habits can you learn or develop that would take you from being a follower to becoming a leader? ▶ *Write for 3 minutes*

4. What resources can you use today that would give you the momentum to get your project started? ▶ *Write for 3 minutes*

Break Barriers

"Only those who dare to fail greatly can achieve greatly."

- Robert Kennedy

After you've made the decision to go after a goal or objective, action is the next key step. When you were first learning to play sports, building your first model airplane, or even applying makeup for the first time, you weren't exactly sure what you were doing. It's a lot like art; being more about the process and then the product. You had a desire, made a decision to do it, and then there was an action you needed to take. Even if it wasn't perfect you took steps to figure it out.

Action is fundamental for moving forward. But decision is the motivator. See, all of us have great ideas. The problem is that many of us keep them inside our heads. So those ideas just keep floating around in there, swimming along with all of the other ideas inside our heads: —Don't forget to put gas in the car. Make a reservation at the restaurant tonight. Create that million dollar board game idea that's the next Monopoly or Life. Remember my wife's birthday. Don't forget to take out the trash tonight. Um... What was my dream again?

Is that you? If it is, there have probably also been times in your life when you made a list on a piece of paper and checked off or crossed out the items you completed. Didn't the simple action of marking off each item feel pretty good to you? Of course it did.

In the past you accomplished a number of goals by structuring your tasks this way and you probably aren't even aware of what they were. First, you needed to get all of those mundane things out of your head. So you created a task list. Doing that freed you up both emotionally and spiritually, and maybe even empowered you a bit. Then you saw your tasks actually getting completed in a timely fashion, and as you checked off each one, it gave you a sense of pride and purpose. Now you knew you could knock off even more projects quicker. And ultimately you created a brand new habit within yourself and new way of thinking. This is exactly what you want.

When listing your tasks in this way, you automatically start to create a *system* in your head to handle and attack them. You first give them an order of importance. Then you create the best method for accomplishment, and now you have a definable mission.

If you've ever worked for someone else, you probably already understand this concept. When you're given an assignment, it's typically written down somewhere. You review it and figure out the best way to get it done. Because your list is tangible and it's not kept just inside your head, you're able to look at it more objectively and begin to figure out the best, most efficient method for completing the tasks to your own level of standards while meeting your employer's wishes.

All of us have done this on some level most of our lives. At some time in your past, you have used a shopping list or a gift list, a to-do list. If you're in business, you're familiar with a call sheet or project list. It becomes something you use as a reference. If you've ever had a call list to manage, you know that you put notes on the call sheet of outstanding issues or phone calls you want to readdress at a later date. Taking action is an important step in the process. The key to make it work best for you is to get your tasks or goals out of your head and onto a piece of paper where you can look at them. This gives you a sense of accomplishment, an ability to set a direction for the next action needed, and a routine that becomes an everyday habit that you do without even thinking about it.

Don't try to cut corners by quickly jotting things on a Post-it and placing a million of these tiny pieces of paper all over your house and/or office. You'll leave them about and forget to review them, and if your eye can't focus on one place you'll never completely focus on your goal. Has this been the case for you? Instead, create a list. The process of writing them all out helps to solidify them in your mind. Actually seeing them on paper also helps to organize them. Checking them off or crossing them out will create a sense of accomplishment. Do not just keep them on your computer. It's okay to type them up on your computer (though writing them by hand creates an even greater connection of importance) to refer to them. Again, this will not be as effective as having something to hold on to, refer to, and check off as you complete each task or project. See each item completed and checking them off is what builds your success muscles.

Top 1% Tip: One multi-million dollar Internet Marketing Entrepreneur not only keeps a daily leather-bound journal of all his thoughts, feelings, and ideas in which he writes every day for over twenty years; he also saves stacks of call logs and journals that even to this day refers to and uses as examples of past experiences and continues to reference for his current objectives. Consistent practice and creating a regular routine of habits brought his small $8 million company to over 80 employees and an annual revenue of $30 million and climbing.

If an athlete - let's say a runner - only watched videos of himself running and never actually ran, he would not have the sense of accomplishment that running will actually give him. While it's true that you can create the same brain patterns of winning by closing your eyes and going through the process of running a race in your mind, and while top athletes do use this method as a part of their success training, this cannot be the only source of training or what's the point? They would ultimately still have to run the race.

Doing the exercise of taking the action and writing something down, then following through, and then marking your task or project as completed, is the best way you are going to form the habits of successful people and train yourself to hit your goal every time.

—— FINISH LINE EXERCISE ——

When you have an idea or a thought, take action IMMEDIATELY!

Even if all you do is just write your ideas down on paper. Taking the smallest step every day will get you miles ahead, and faster than you've ever traveled before. For example, if your goal is to write a book and your action is to write just one page a day, you'll have thirty pages completed after just one month. Once you get started, you'll quickly find it doesn't take an entire day to write one page. As you become more disciplined, you can then make it your goal to write six pages a day. At this rate you can write an entire book in a month.

List 10 ideas or thoughts you've been keeping inside your head:

1.   6.

2.   7.

3.   8.

4.   9.

5.   10.

—— FINISH LINE EXERCISE *continued* ——

Choose 3 of these ideas or goals and decide on an action you'll take towards reaching them (Remember even the smallest of actions can create massive forward movement):

1.

2.

3.

Pick 1 of the 3 goals or ideas and for one week take 5 actions every day towards that goal or idea (Small actions, big rewards):

Daily Example (Monday) : _____

1.

2.

3.

4.

5.

TIP: Put a reminder on your cell phone that pops up and tells you to take 5 actions every day.

It's A New Day

"Have a bigger vision for your life. There are exciting things in your future."

 - Joel Osteen

By taking the action of reading this book, you've already started to build a new habit. Within the pages of this book are some important methods for magnifying the actions you take. You're never too young to be successful, or too old to start something new.

Case in point: In my early thirties, I was seeking a position to be a junior copywriter at an ad firm. My competition was early twenties, and I was afraid I wouldn't get the position because I lacked youth. On the contrary, I was hired because I was older, which to the senior copywriter translated into *life* experience. I had so many things to bring to the table because I'd experienced life and knew what people just like myself wanted. I understood the pain and necessity of having to earn my own money so I was more conscientious about what experience I brought to the table, which was exactly what the agency wanted so they could figure out how better to market to people like myself.

For example, I had driven and owned several cars by that time, so I knew what I was looking for versus only going for the shiny elements of purchasing an automobile (although shiny was important, too). I was a seasoned traveler, I had paid lots of rent and many bills, was a shopper and consumer, and succeeded and failed at life several times over. All of these factors helped give me insight into the people we marketed to. So the point is, it is never too late.

Later, I became a high-level Personal Assistant for some of the most successful and creative people in the United States. And even though I'm not at liberty to say exactly who I worked for during my 15 years in that field, I can tell you that many of the people I served were and remain household names. I had hit the top of my field! And again, I started late in life. Most career Personal Assistants began in their early twenties.

Now, once again, late in life, I've taken on a new direction - as a speaker and trainer.

I don't believe in using age as an excuse. I took up mixed martial arts in my forties, competing and training against some seriously strong, youthful, agile, tough kids who had years of experience over me. I even sustained more bruises than I cared to have, and had my thumb broken for the first time. But I stuck with it and learned because I desired a new level of self-improvement and wanted to live a life of no limits.

Of course, not everyone is going to be interested in some of the things I've gone after. That's not my point here. The point is that you may have kept some great, amazing ideas inside of your head for many years thinking now that it's too late to start. It's never too late. But don't get me wrong: the clock won't stop for you. It's going to keep on ticking, and you need to figure out how passionate you really are about what you want. Make a decision that this is your time and that now is the right moment to make your dreams and goals a reality.

Age and lack of time are never good excuses for why you shouldn't start. Abraham Lincoln didn't become President until he was 52 years old, in 1861. Henry Ford was 38 when he formed the Ford Motor Company. Winston Churchill didn't become Prime Minister until the age of 66. So now that age is no longer an excuse for you, what is your next immediate step to put your plans and ideas into action?

Top 1% Tip: After being a successful Television Producer of several Emmy-winning shows, building and running a major studio, building hospitals, and resorts, at 73 years old this successful man went into yet another direction funding and supporting a major Temple whose mission of peace and goodwill continue to influence and effect positive change in the world. Through persistence and networking he became a top influential player.

Being too young is also not an excuse you can use to justify why you aren't fully pursuing your goals. I've heard people say they don't know enough. Enough can always be learned. Some have said they're not smart enough. I say to them build a team of people who do know and can teach you or show you the way. People love to help if asked. I've heard the excuse of not having enough financial resources. When you want it enough you can always find a way. When starting this company I had three thousand dollars to my name and my rent was two thousand. The answer? Put the message out there. Create a dream or goal or a desire that is genuine and that others can resonate with. If you are a hard working, good person of ambition and integrity, you will be shown ways to get there as long as you keep moving forward. You cannot wait for someone to come along and rescue you. You must show them your desire of your goals through your intention, integrity, and hard work. Only then will others offer their advice and assistance.

I've had people tell me they aren't gifted or as lucky as others. There is no such thing as luck. There is only passion, drive, and intention. And as long as all three are used for good and you are adding value to your life and the lives of others, you will become gifted by the opportunities and people who come into your life and help you to reach the dream you envision so clearly. You are never too young or too old to have and pursue a dream. Instead, place in your mind that you are too creative and passionate to let anything stand between you and the finish line.

—— FINISH LINE EXERCISE ——

▶ What is the best way to accomplished your tasks?

▶ What is the fastest way?

▶ How do you get the clutter out of your head so you are left with only reaching your goal?

CREATE A TASK LIST

Limit it to no more than 7-10 items.

This can be chores, errands, tasks, or goals.

☐ 1.　　　　　　　　　☐ 6.

☐ 2.　　　　　　　　　☐ 7.

☐ 3.　　　　　　　　　☐ 8.

☐ 4.　　　　　　　　　☐ 9.

☐ 5.　　　　　　　　　☐ 10.

As you complete each one, **check** them off then **cross** them out. This will create a sense of COMPLETION within you and you'll look forward to doing this more and more.

If you have one or two tasks left by the end of the day, create a brand new list for tomorrow. You always want to start with a fresh list. WARNING: If you carry over a list with cross-outs on it for several days you will go back to a feeling of non-accomplishment.

—— FINISH LINE EXERCISE *continued* ——

REMOVING THE LIMITATIONS:

You will be given this exercise several times throughout the book.

If you had no limitations placed upon you (financial, health, time, career, or family), what would you dare to dream?

▶ Do you see yourself wearing smaller clothes?

▶ Going to the beach in a sexy outfit?

▶ Working for yourself?

▶ Leaving your job for the position of your dreams?

▶ Finding a better place to live?

What would you dare to dream if you could not fail?

Top 1% Tip: To become a Grammy winning, world renown singer, this successful performer had to first get out there and perform in the smallest of venues where she worked out her music and continued to build a small following . As her momentum built, others of influence took notice of her and soon she was performing on major tours all over the world, on radio, TV and in movies. Her willingness to continue to perfect her craft and perfect her skills paid off for this icon.

You Can't Be Contained

"If you can dream it, you can do it."

- Walt Disney

When you start to get momentum on your projects you feel more energy, you feel more alive and things start to fall into place. We've all had those days when everything happens perfectly, almost seamlessly. You hit your stride every time and it feels almost simple - like you're finally getting it, you're in the groove, on a roll. It's weird how you couldn't tap into this process earlier. But once you develop a taste for how good this feels, you want more. And you want to keep experiencing that same drive and energy from within. Some people may even choose to wake up earlier as a result of their progress.

Momentum is an important part of the process in reaching your goals. And the best way to get unstoppable momentum is to begin by taking the littlest steps. It was Martin Luther King Jr. who said; "Faith is taking the first step even when you don't see the whole staircase". When you step on the gas pedal in a car, you don't get to 60 miles per hour right away. You build up momentum that makes it go faster. When you ski down a hill it's your increasing momentum that gives you speed. When you take action after action as you go toward your goal, you increase the rate at which your accomplishments get completed. At first, anything new is going to be slow going. But as you complete every new task, repetition and familiarity will build up your momentum. When you repeat something over and over until it becomes a habit to you, you create confidence. With this confidence, you begin to explore and expand your boundaries. Remember the first time you used a kitchen knife and how careful you were? Over time, your muscles and brain remembered the movement and action, the way you held the knife just so, the way you placed the knuckles of your other hand for cutting accuracy and size. And after a while you began cutting and chopping a little faster. You began to try different types of knives and varied your techniques. You became bolder, because using a kitchen knife became a part of your identity.

It's the same way when you begin a new job. At first you go slowly and then you get into a groove and begin to feel more comfortable and confident. Soon you're able to see ways to make your job more efficient, more productive, and you get things done at a faster rate. It's the same for driving, rearing children, dating, and sports. The more you do something, the deeper into your muscle and brain memory the routine becomes ingrained. Soon you find you're discovering newer and even better ways to perform. Singing and playing a musical instrument are like this too. Suddenly you're trying riffs and accents you've never attempted before. You notice that you're beginning to create your own style and flavor. How can you be contained when you feel so comfortable, so natural at what you do? And the first step towards making anything a part of you is to take action.

—— FINISH LINE EXERCISE ——

Think hard. If you had no financial constraints, if there were no health concerns, if you didn't have to worry about a job, and if there were no family obligations, what would you DARE to DREAM?

▶ What is your BIG goal?

▶ Why do you think this is your goal? (Take 10 minutes to write out your thinking process)

—— FINISH LINE EXERCISE *continued*——

▶ What would achieving this goal do for you? (and how would it change you?)

Most people think they have a goal when their goal is really something different. By really funneling down why you think this is your goal and what's behind your thought process, you can then come up with what truly may be your real goal.

$600,000 Example:

When told that someone had a goal of having $600,000, the first and most obvious question is, why? What would you do with the money?

After some thinking the answer was; "So I could travel."

"But what if I showed you how to travel on $500 and live like a king? Would you still need the $600,000?"

"No." Was the obvious answer.

Slowly the real reason started to unravel. After some deeper searching, the thought process was that this person felt stuck at their job and having the $600,000 would allow them the freedom to become independent and no longer have to stay at a job they did not like and they felt was holding them back.

So the real goal was not about the money at all. The *real goal* was freedom from their job.

Be First In Line

"Shoot for the moon. Even if you miss, you'll land among the stars."

- Les Brown

We all know that being first in line gets you the best seats at a concert. The best seats at a movie. The best job. The best parking space. But what does it mean to be first in line in every area of your life? To be first in line means that the passions you develop through taking action are becoming greater than the pain of doing nothing at all and staying in your old routine and behaviors.

You can create the habit within yourself to be first in line. When you think of calling someone, do it right away. When you think about writing something down, don't wait for a better time - do it immediately. When you have a new project, no matter how big, do one thing towards reaching it every day, as soon as you think of it. The biggest of good intentions cannot compare with the smallest of actions.

To create new patterns of success, don't just get in line. Rush to the front. Being first in line is telling yourself that you are someone who is great at goal setting. Whatever you go after is well within your reach. It tells others that you are determined and focused. You start to see new and better ways to get things accomplished, and with every accomplishment you empower yourself more each day.

Being first in line can be scary. But it's exciting, too. I don't know how many speakers I've met who told me that after many years of speaking in front of audiences from 50 to 4,000 people, they still get nervous or afraid. The difference is that they don't act upon that fear.

Top 1% Tip: This Venture Capitalist acted immediately on his tasks and projects with little hesitation, creating a pattern that caused investors to take him very seriously. They saw that his immediate call to action created results that beat out his competition time and again bringing his business to outstanding levels of success. Investors tripled their investments consistently backed by his ability to quickly make a decision and take immediate action.

Several years ago there's an actress who was a guest on the "Tonight Show" with Jay Leno. She always seemed to live life at its fullest, always happy, alive, and excited to meet and talk with people. She was someone that others naturally gravitated to, and it was clear that others wanted to be around her. And Jay picked up on this. So he asked her, what is it that she does that makes her live life to its fullest? How come she seems to handle everything so much better than other people? Was it her family upbringing? Was it luck? Did she posses a skill that other people did not? Why did this amazing woman, this successful movie star, live life at such a high level?

She indicated with her index finger for Jay to come in closer for the answer, as if this was going to be an intimate secret between him and her, even though she knew that millions of viewers were also watching her, listening and hanging onto her every word waiting for this secret that catapulted her to the top of her game. Her answer? She realized long ago that everyone on some level was self-conscious about how others saw themselves and that she too felt that way. The difference was that she never acted upon it.

Never let your fears surface long enough to set in. When self-doubt entered this actress's mind, she never acted on it. Instead she went in the opposite direction. For example, if she thought it would be foolish or embarrassing to go up and speak with someone she admired, instead of thinking it was stupid or would only end in disaster, she immediately approached that person. And more times than not, she found that the other person was interested in meeting her too. In fact, most of the time, taking these risks in her life helped her rocket into the successful career she has today. At some point in her life she made the determination not to sit on the sidelines. If she wanted to move forward in her life and career, she was going to have to push her hesitations and doubts aside and never act on them again!

Being first in line simply means taking action now and not waiting. The rewards are huge. Being first in line motivates you to want more from yourself.

—— FINISH LINE EXERCISE ——

Learn to take immediate action in everything you do!

▶ List 5 actions you can take right now to get your goal kick-started.

1.

2.

3.

4.

5.

▶ What decision will you make TODAY to get your goal off the ground?

Decide if your goal is the result of a true passion you have. (this will help you see it become a reality), or if you are someone who is in so much pain about your current situation that you must make a change for the better. *(Example: You want to get control of your weight or poor eating habits. You are not happy with your current job and feel stuck like there's no place to go).*

REMOVING THE LIMITATIONS: You will be given this exercise several times throughout the book –If you had no limitations placed upon you (financial, health, time, career, or family), what would you dare to dream? Do you see yourself wearing smaller clothes? Going to the beach in a sexy outfit? Working for yourself? Leaving your job for the position of your dreams? Getting a better place to live?

▶ What would you dare to dream?

Making Your Mark

"It's kinda fun to do the impossible."

- Walt Disney

So what is it that you want to accomplish? And why haven't you already hit your goal? Einstein said that "Imagination is much more important than intelligence." And while that's true, the real mark you leave is what you do with that imagination. Did you simply keep your great idea locked up in the attic of your mind for several years and let it get dusty? You may have the challenge of feeling overwhelmed by having so many great ideas and not knowing where to start and how to unlock them from inside your head.

Shari was just like that. Over the years, she's had tons of really great ideas over the years. And yet every year she was no closer to pulling the trigger on any of them. Every year the thought of them weighed her down more and more as she kept piling newer ones on top of the old, creating more fear and anxiety as each action-less year passed by. Boy, her head must weigh a ton! It was only when I gave her an exercise to tackle only one goal at a time by taking one action at a time, that the simplicity of getting them all accomplished started to take root. By taking that simple mind shift, her journey towards finishing what she started actually became a reality.

As I'm writing this, she has a children's book that's almost finished and two business ideas that are now on their way to being successful ventures. And it all started with a commitment to action.

By attacking just one goal at a time and taking that first step, you can achieve similar success.

Making your mark is less about how others perceive and remember you, and more about how you perceive yourself; what you choose to do with your life, and does it add to the world around you.

Where you come from and any lack of opportunity is a thing of the past. It's been proven over and over again by thousands of individuals from poor environments who have a dream and yet they've overcome the obstacles around them. And it had little to do with the opportunities that were available to them. It's about creating a clear vision within yourself and working every day towards reaching your goal.

And for these people, their imaginations were not limited by their situations. In fact, the opposite is true. It's their imagination and the free-flowing thinking they allowed themselves that brought them out of their current situation to rise high above, then help others to do the same. So dare to dream. Dream big. And when you see it within you, find a way to begin your journey to make it real. It can't exist out here in the real world until you build it within your imagination.

Ask yourself this question; what would you dream up if you knew you could not fail?

Take a moment to really think about and explore this question. Then get out a pen and paper and write your answers down.

Increase Your Influence

"You cannot teach a man anything; you can only help him to find it within himself."

- Galileo Galilei

Voltaire wrote: "By appreciation, we make excellence in others our own property." I love that phrase. Have you ever noticed how other people can influence you through the example they set? You've probably had the experience of seeing a friend or associate do something you thought was unattainable in a way that was really simple for them. Did you also notice how all your stress and worry around that same goal suddenly seemed to vanish through their success? It is because of their influence that you saw that you too could accomplish the same objectives by using the same drive and passion!

When someone sees you taking action towards your goals, they too will get motivated and inspired. It's why we listen to great speakers, read motivational stories, and watch television shows of inspirational feats. We get motivated when we learn about someone else who triumphed over struggle. It's empowering to watch another person succeed and reach the finish line. It is why we have heroes. It's also why fictional superheroes without the use of super powers - like Batman and Ironman - are so much more compelling than those with super powers. This could be your story! We love when someone who's a lot like us has overcome great odds and survived - or better yet, improved their life!

There are people like Morris Goodman, a Texan who survived a plane crash he wasn't "supposed" to, and then used the power of his will to build his strength after doctors told him he would be paralyzed for the rest of his life. Goodman, was one of the featured teachers in the hit video "The Secret". He astounded his skeptics when he walked out of the hospital on his own two feet - just like he said he would.

Kevin Saunders was just like any other young man from the Kansas countryside. Fresh out of college and starting a family, he worked long hours as a Federal grain elevator inspector. Touring facilities day after day in the heat, he knew the job wouldn't be easy -but he didn't know it would nearly take his life.

But then, on a busy afternoon like any other, Kevin heard the sound he would never forget ... one explosion, and then another, snapping like popcorn in the distance. The rising volume and tremor of the floor told an unmistakable truth - that the building he was standing in would soon burst into flames. And, in a matter of seconds, it did. Before he had time to even think or move, a blast rocketed the office and sent him over a 2-story building three hundred feet into the air. When rescuers found him, he was lying a quarter of a mile away in a parking lot, bent and broken at the chest.

For days, Kevin lay teetering on the edge of life and death, even hearing his doctor admit to a visitor that there "wasn't any hope." Against all odds, he survived his injuries only to find that the real trauma was about to begin. Paralyzed from the chest down, he struggled to find a new meaning and focus for his life. Abused and abandoned by his young wife, his life fell into disarray. Divorced, bankrupt, and utterly alone, Kevin fell into a deep depression.

But rather than remain miserable, Kevin did what he now teaches audiences around the world to do - he decided to keep moving forward. By sharpening his body and mind together, he became a world class competitor. Athletically, he won hundreds of gold medals and earned the title of "the greatest all-around wheelchair athlete in the world." And that success was only the beginning. He's gone on to feature in a major motion picture, serve under two administrations on the President's Council on Physical Fitness, participate in "the biggest turnaround in college sports history," push his wheelchair across North America and Europe, and even pen five books and appear on shows like ESPN, USA Today and countless other national, international and local media outlets.

You too can be a great motivator to others. And your influence can also be infectious. We'd rather catch inspiration than a cold any day. We as a society are always looking for the magic bullet or the secret key that unlocks the doors to success. When we see others who are successfully doing what we want to do, we look to them for influence and inspiration so we too can duplicate their success and reach our full potential.

There may be times when you feel alone or isolated in your mission to reach your goals. You might think no one is aware of your situation. You may be surprised to learn that you may be influencing friends and family who are watching you walk through the maze, observing how you are learning and figuring out how to get on the right path and achieve your goals.

It never ceases to surprise me when I think I'm going through something totally on my own, only to find out that a family member or friend has been inspired by my working through each and every step. They are amazed that I am constantly moving forward even when it seems at times like I'm hitting walls. But like drilling for oil, you're bound to hit rock every now and then. It's what you do once you hit that rock that determines your fate. The next steps you take are the ones everyone waits and watches for. Once you figure out how to overcome that obstacle, they too will now have the same tools through your example, and the power of momentum to move forward.

Let me further illustrate what I mean. There was a time when no one could break the four-minute mile. It just couldn't be done, the experts said. Then one day, in 1954, Roger Banister did just that. He achieved what others simply thought was not achievable. Then what happened? Just 46 days later, other runners had beaten that record time. And they kept getting faster and faster.

In every field, we see the same story repeated. When Charles Lindbergh crossed the Atlantic in the Spirit of St. Louis, it was clear to everyone that the limits of travel were redefined when it came to how far a plane could safely venture overseas. In that same vein, there was the inception of the Piggly-Wiggly supermarket concept. Once they honed the supermarket model in a time when everything else was general stores that relied on delivery, they streamlined the process and increased their customer base. Soon others followed. Another example of setting the standard was the Wright Brothers who successfully built the first working aero plane. Ray Kroc was a leader in refining the franchise concept with his McDonalds business. Starbucks came up with a new coffee shop concept and soon others followed suit. Think about how small data storage for computers has become in just a couple decades. In the beginning the storage units were massive, with giant reels of tape. Once someone figured out a new method of storage, it opened up opportunities for others to improve the concept even more and create smaller and faster means of storage while the capacity grew.

Taking this even a step further, let's look at an example of how groups can also add value. Can you remember what communication was like before the World Wide Web was developed at CERN? CERN is the European Organization for Nuclear Research. The name is derived from the acronym for the French Conseil Européen pour la Recherche Nucléaire, or European Council for Nuclear Research. This organization whose primary goal is to seek out and find answers to questions about the universe, made sure the Web would be free for everyone to use, and will always remain so. Their influence in that decision was infectious, and still is. While there are companies that try to privatize certain inventions and hold us hostage to their use, CERN took a step towards opening the field.

As a result, more information is shared and readily available to you than ever before. And additionally, more people have benefited from it. Socially it has had a huge impact. More jobs, opportunities, and inventions have become a reality as a result of this incredible entity that is free to us all. We've become closer to each other thanks to the information that can be shared around the entire globe. We know things about other countries that in the past were a mystery to many of us. We have new forms of entertainment, knowledge, and social and economic influences than ever before. And all because CERN decided to make this invention free to everyone.

CERN's influence was never about controlling or mastering others. It was about growing their relationships and bringing even more people together. They wanted to level the playing field and give everyone an equal opportunity to thrive granting everyone access to the same information.

There are of course other very successful businesses and inventions that were private, are making a great deal of money, but they also help to create thousands of new jobs and positions. As well as, new fields of endeavor, and opened the market up to new ideas and ventures. Two such successful businesses are MTV and Google. And while MTV is not what it once was, you cannot dispute the influence and impact it's had and continues to have on both the music and television industries.

Choose Your Tomorrow

"Dream as if you'll live forever. Live as if you'll die today."

- James Dean

There are more resources available today than at any other time in history. You can make whatever you can think up become a reality. You are limited only by your imagination and actions.

Even with the illusion of scarce resources, your imagination and action are the only two tools that may hold you back.

What happens when you have a bill that's looming? You either find a way to pay it or you make an arrangement. Let's say you don't have the cash on hand to pay your bill, and you don't make an arrangement to pay it. What happens then? If you try to ignore that bill, it can overwhelm your very thoughts to the point that you can't think about anything but that bill. The impact of that looming debt grows like a virus. You now start to worry about credit problems. You can't see beyond this immediate problem. You're afraid to answer the phone or open the mailbox. Its negative impact becomes greater and greater.

Then one day, you're in so much pain and discomfort, you decide that no matter how bad this is, you decided it won't kill you. You may feel overwhelmed, frustrated, and upset. You may feel shut down emotionally and energetically. But you're still here.

You eventually find a way to get beyond the situation. You either figured out a way to pay your debt, ignored it, which some people do, and you learned that you were still able to go on and move forward.

At one point in my life I had looming debts totaling more than $60,000. Without a job or steady income at that time, I did everything I could to run from them. I stopped answering my phone. I immediately threw all unopened mail away. I hid from debt collectors in every way I could think of. I remember going to the movies in the daytime, only seeing comedies so I could have something to smile about, at least for a little while. But I was a mess. I was even afraid that I'd come out of the theater and a debt collector would be there, waiting for me.

However, a funny thing happened. A year later, while I still had all this looming debt I noticed that I was still intact. I could still get up; I could still eat, bathe, dress, and go out into the world. I soon began to realize that any powers this debt had over me was only in my head. And that's when I changed my outlook.

I started to open all the bills that came to me and I made a list of my outstanding debts. By this time some of them had grown because of interest, and my total debt was now closer to $80,000. Still, I decided to take control over this. I typed a list of all of my debts on my computer and printed them out in order from the smallest amount on top all the way down to the largest debt at the bottom of the page. Then I called each collector and asked if there was anything I could do to get them paid without taking forty years and all my finances to do so.

Some wouldn't budge, while others lowered their interest rates putting me on what they called a "hardship program." Some had gone to collections and they would take a reduction in the amount owed because now they owned the account for pennies on the dollar and they just wanted to make some money back. A creditor I owed $2,000 was willing to accept $1,200, which was good news for me. And then when I discovered that I could tell them even that amount of money was too much of a struggle for me, some agencies were willing to knock off even more - as much as a few hundred dollars more.

So I reworked my debt sheet and put the ones with the highest interest on top, and then the reduced interest ones, then the collections accounts, unless there was a timeframe in which I had to pay these back. Then, I began attacking these debts.

Using a concept that David Bach perfected in his book *Start Over, Finish Rich*, I pulled out all my bill statements and wrote down the names, amounts I owed, and the minimum payments required, along with the due date of every bill. He suggests dividing the balance by the minimum monthly payment. In other words, if my outstanding balance on one account is $1,000 and the minimum monthly payment is $50, then by dividing that I come up with 20. He calls this number the DOLP number. I also had to make sure I was conscious of the due date for every outstanding bill (you do not want to miss your due date, EVER). Then I assigned a ranking to each bill. Order doesn't matter, but I decided to attack the highest interest rates first. Then, as David suggests, I paid the minimum monthly payment for every bill except the very first one in the ranking system. For this one, he suggests paying as much as you can (no less than double the minimum due) until it's paid off. So again, if I have an outstanding balance of $1,000 and the minimum monthly payment is $50 it would take me 20 payments to pay this off. However, if I double my payments on the first DOLP account, it brings it down to only 10 payments (or less if I decide to pay more every month).

Once my debts were no longer overpowering me and holding me prisoner I began to get creative and figure out ways to knock them down even faster. Part of this was selling off things I simply did not need, like complete DVD sets of shows like Friends and The Pretender. I sold old cell phones I had laying around, put clothes on consignment, and everything I hadn't used in the past six months. I became determined to overcome this, like a warrior. The motivation spurred by my actions to overcome the situation got me even more determined. I got a part-time job for a few hours on the weekends, and I volunteered my services at places, always asking if they were looking to hire. In six months I knocked my debt almost in half. I spent less on entertainment and ate at home more. I even came to count on the grace of my friends to feed and cook for me to save even more money - which, by the way, they were happy to do when they found out the reasons why.

One year later I had only twenty-thousand dollars in debt left and by that time I was able to start doing more fun things and adding entertainment back into my life. It's not like the pleasurable things ever went away completely. Friends would take me to the movies or concerts or have me over to their houses. We came up with free, creative ways to have fun. So it wasn't like all the fun had gone out of my life. But now I was able to pay for some of it. I was no longer contained by my financial situation.

During this time my creativity started to come back with a passion. I wrote a handbook for Personal Assistants which started selling great. Since I was more empowered I worked harder for my bosses and it showed and soon my income and value went up. I was no longer being contained.

Actually, any containment I experienced was of my own doing. It was all in my mind. The stress and pressure I created was what really kept me down. The creditors weren't holding me prisoner, I was!

You Have What You Need Right Now

"If you deliberately plan on being less than you are capable of being, then I warn you that you'll be unhappy for the rest of your life."

   - Abraham Maslow

Everyone has within them the capacity to either create great success in their life or to fail. We always have. So why do some people seem to have an easier time moving up the ladder than others? There's a saying: People who succeed do not have fewer problems than those who fail. So what exactly are the differences between those who are successful and those who simply desire to be successful?

Before we delve deeper I want to state here that success does not only mean monetary fulfillment. While we as a society view this as an indicator of success, it's only one aspect of many. Throughout this entire book, the attainment of success will also encompass areas of personal achievement, career aspirations, health and fitness objectives, romantic endeavors, and creative goals.

The first way to truly understand this better is to look at the belief systems successful people have. People who succeed have a solid core conviction that they're going to accomplish their goals. Often, they are not sure how they're going to get there - they just have a solid faith that they will.

Beliefs either empower us and free us to achieve even more ("limitless" beliefs) or limit us by our accepting them ("limiting" beliefs). And most of us have a number of limiting beliefs - whether it comes to our careers, our incomes, how we interact with others and the kind of people we feel comfortable around. How many limiting beliefs about yourself can you come up with right now? My guess is quite a few.

It's been said that the average person has sixty-thousand thoughts per day and that eighty percent of those are negative. The source quoted is said to be the National Science Foundation (NSF) but I've researched this extensively and cannot substantiate it. However, let's go on the presumption for the moment that this statement is true.

Now, try to come up with five *limitless* beliefs about yourself. Just five.

If you're like most people, you've found it's a bit hard. Why is that? Why should we have more powerless thoughts about ourselves, and what we are not capable of, than the empowering ones?

There are moments in all of our lives when we have had a limiting belief about our capabilities, and then somehow we did the very thing we thought we couldn't do. Try and recall such a moment right now. It may have been about starting a new job at an age when you thought you were too old. Maybe you took up a new hobby that you never felt you would end up being any good at. At first, you thought it might be a fluke that it went well. But what was really behind your triumph? You made a conscious decision to go after something and then you took the action towards obtaining it. Perhaps you thought you would never get that raise but you asked anyway - and you got it. Or you asked someone out on a date whom you thought was "out of your league" and they said yes. Maybe you wanted to lose a little weight and you succeeded.

We all have moments in our lives when this has occurred for us. In each of these instances the key element was that you made a conscious decision towards achieving that goal you thought was out of your reach. You didn't know how you'd get there or what the results would be, but you took the action and it worked. (There are also examples of times when it didn't turn out in your favor, which we'll address later on.)

Our belief system about what we're capable of is predicated partly on the number of successes and failures we have had in our lives. But more importantly, they are also predicated on whether you tried or not. Again, decision and action are the key.

So why don't we take the chance and act on everything we want to? For most of us, fear comes into play. Some people worry about and become embarrassed if things don't work out. Some don't feel they have a high level of self-esteem to weather a failure. The fear of embarrassment is a powerful force in many people's lives. And for almost all of us fear can be debilitating.

What kind of impact can a debilitating fear have on one's life? People who have agoraphobia are almost incapacitated by the simplest of tasks most of us take for granted, like going outside. There are people who fear being judged, criticized, or get so embarrassed they often don't make an effort to try. They have decided in their mind that others will look down upon them and ridicule or ostracize them in public. For some that feeling is unbearable. So to support the seemingly safe world that they have built for themselves, their belief system says that it is better not to take action. If they remain quiet, don't draw attention to themselves, they will simply exist in this supposedly safe environment they have created for themselves. But, their lives will never reach the maximization of passion, love, success, and incredible memories.

So how does someone form a positive belief? By making decisions, and taking action. Action does some wonderful things for our psyches. When you first take an action there are two roads you can travel down. One is success, however big or small. And the other, of course, is failure. But what really happens when you experience failure? Your life is not over. The world did not end. You simply did not achieve your desired results. And when you don't achieve the results you want or expect, what do you do? Try again. Rarely does someone give up after their first attempt. When you dial a phone and you get the number wrong, do you stop dialing or never use the phone again? No. You do it again until you get the desired results. How many times in your life have you misdialed? And while this is a very simplistic example, dialing the wrong phone number isn't all that different from any other failure in life. Why? It is important to distinguish what caused the results when you dialed the wrong number. Again, it's in the decision to do it and the action you took. And then you readjusted your tactics until you got the outcome you desired. Then what happened? Your belief system changed. You now had the belief that when you slowed down and consciously dialed a phone number even after several tries; you found that you could get the results you wanted.

On a slightly larger scale, many of us have driven a stick shift or manual transmission car at some point in our lives. Can you remember what that was like in the beginning? At first it was frustrating, and perhaps even a bit embarrassing. Popping the clutch. Stalling out the car and having other drivers honk their horns in frustration at you. But did you quit? No. Because while it may have been an embarrassing moment, it wasn't something that caused a great deal of anxiety within you. You attempted to master it. In fact, like most people, you were determined to conquer this and practice until it became part of you. You also saw through example how fun it was for others once they mastered it. Your belief system changed, and you became more confident with each success you had driving that stick shift. This small success ignited your ability to venture out even further, and attempt to try various new things in your life.

Top 1% Tip: This A-list Actress had failed more times than even she cared to remember. Through continued readjustments in her methods and tactics, she is today a household name. She has more long running hit shows than most of her peers (all still airing today), and she continues to work successfully in movies and TV. Her tenacity and drive are the foundation of her success.

We try new things all the time, every day, and in ways we're sometimes not even aware of. We do it with seemingly small things, like learning to use a DVD player or working a new remote control. Cooking for the first time. Washing clothes for the first time. Throwing your first party. Going on your first trip. Applying for your first job. Having a baby for the first time! We all believe that these things may not turn out well, but we still take the action towards them. Then readjust our methods if it didn't go as planned at the first attempt. But did we stop trying new things? No, because we knew that none of these things were life threatening, and that others have done it before us. So because someone else had positive results, we knew that it was possible for us to create the same environment and duplicate the same results. Therefore changing our belief system created more and more positive results in our minds as our successes began to add up.

Now that you've seen some examples of how your beliefs and your success influence each other, I'd like to ask you again about your *limiting* and *limitless* beliefs.

For me the (past) limiting beliefs were:

- I'd always be poor

- I wasn't smart

- I would always be single

- I'd never be successful

- I wouldn't fit in

My positive beliefs became:

- I'm very creative

- I'm extremely driven

- I'm smart and as long as I remain open, I can learn anything I put my mind and effort into

- I'm a money magnet

- I'm someone who is a valuable, passionate, healthy, fun, exciting partner

- I'm a great teacher and love being around positive people

- I have an amazing, successful business that I'm incredibly passionate about

It's a bit easier now, isn't it?

So what's the formula here? First, recognize that you can and do possess positive beliefs. Second, making a decision along with taking an action are key elements to having a desirable outcome. Third, recognize that it's more than likely that other people have been successful at whatever you too desire to achieve. And lastly, understand that you are never less of a person when you don't succeed. In fact, you're a better person for taking the action.

One of the other *Power Principles* we're going to talk about later on is how you can use other people to help you maximize your success rate in everything you attempt. Maximizing your success is, of course, why you're reading this book in the first place! You want to have more success in your life and *finish what you start.*

—— FINISH LINE EXERCISE ——

▶ Write down 5 things that you've had limiting beliefs about.

▶ Then list 5 things which you've had positive beliefs about.

A limiting belief is something you have doubts or hesitations about. Typically there is a fear that's the reason behind your limiting feelings.

Try to identify what's behind these limiting beliefs and where they originated. What is your past has told you that you are not capable of reaching beyond those limitations?

TIP: For your limiting beliefs, think back to a time when you felt alone or where you are at a place that you weren't performing at your peak.

▶ **LIST 5 LIMITING BELIEFS:**

1.

2.

3.

4.

5.

—— FINISH LINE EXERCISE *continued* ——

▶ **LIST 5 POSITIVE BELIEFS:**

1.

2.

3.

4.

5.

There is no one to review or give you feedback on your answers so dig deep and think about what you really believe you are capable of, then take it a step farther.

Example: If you think you would like to have a net worth of one million dollars, why stop there? Why aren't you worth ten million dollars?

Tip: For your positive (limitless) beliefs take off all restraints. If you knew that there was no way you could fail, what would your beliefs be?

New Levels Of Your Destiny

"To achieve goals you must set them."

- Brian Tracy

S uccess, whether big or small, creates a new sense of *self* and a higher level of *self*. When we achieve, we evolve. When our development accelerates we pick up momentum in our lives. Some tasks will become easier, and some become more fulfilling.

We'll still face challenges, but challenges are part of the process because we're reaching higher than ever before and with great reward there's always a learning curve. As you master this new skill, your mind is creating memory maps that recognize previous accomplishments. Based on this memory mapping that level of success is well within your reach. As a result, you become more daring, more powerful, more willing to extend your comfort zone and take greater risks.

Every time you venture outside of your comfort zone, you create a foundation for growth and courage in your convictions. You still may not know what your destiny is or where life will take you yet, but you're now up for the challenge. It's why we choose to take classes and read more books. It's why we enjoy venturing out to a new movie or dining at a new restaurant. It's why we talk to someone while waiting in line at the bank or supermarket. You are evolving into someone better, someone more fulfilled.

What Is Fear And How To Overcome It

"There are two ways to live your life. One is as though nothing is a miracle. The other is as if everything is."

  - Albert Einstein

A s I've mentioned earlier, life doesn't stop. Time keeps moving forward. So if you think about it, in many ways you're already extending your comfort zone.

Every second, every minute, every hour, of every day, we recalibrate and take one more step outside our area of comfort to test the waters. We have to or we wouldn't survive for very long.

Even those with the biggest fears are at some point in their lives challenged to try something new. The difference is that some will choose to never try again, and some will try it several times more before making a decision whether it works for them. Some will create faster, better ways to adjust, and venture even farther outside their comfort zone. Whatever your level of comfort, one of the key components to growth is how you decide to process your individual results and what you choose to do with that information.

There are tons of reasons to not stretch your comfort zone. And they all boil down to fear. Any time someone decides not to take action towards reaching his or her dreams and goals, it typically comes down to the fact that fear has once again reared its ugly head.

Anxiety... it's fear.

Hesitation... it's fear.

Resistance… it's fear.

Shyness… fear.

Embarrassment… again, it's fear.

So just how many types of fear are there?

Well, you might be surprised to learn that there are only six basic types of fear:

- Poverty
- Old Age
- Criticism
- Loss or Lack of Love
- Ill-Health
- Death

These are the basic fears that surround everything we find a reason not to do in life. You never really completely overcome fear. Even the most experienced and successful people can experience some form of fear at different times in their lives. In fact, some of the greatest speakers I know confess that they still have anxiety when going on stage in front of an audience.

The solution? Well for this one I have to take my hat off to Susan Jeffers, Ph. D. author of the book "Feel The Fear And Do It Anyway."

That's right. When you get anxious, scared, nervous, or you get the sweats, you still go forward and do what's in front of you.

And the reward? After several times, the experience won't feel so bad. What's the worst that happens? Embarrassment? Ridicule? You fall flat on your face? Okay. But let me ask you this? Did you survive?

And did you know that everyone experiences these anxieties? You're not alone here. If you think you are, go to a bookstore sometime and see just how many books there are on the subject. If you were the only one, publishers would lose their shirts.

Now there are some things you may not be able to just walk through, like illness and death. But let's look at both of those for a moment.

When you experience illness, the feeling of not being a whole person capable of taking care of yourself can be overwhelming. We all desire our independence - in being a capable, self-sufficient person who can contribute to society, and not having to rely on society to take care of us.

But we don't always get a choice. Ill-health can come from heredity. Or it can be from an accident. There are also cases of people who have served in war and now have problems and symptoms that debilitate them.

One of the keys here is, whenever possible, not to wait until your symptoms of fear have grown beyond what's reasonable before you take action towards them. It's necessary not to let something go too long before you find ways to remedy the problem.

In Canada, England, France, parts of Spain, and a few other countries, they practice what's called preventative medicine, where the doctors actually are rewarded for having fewer patients who require care and attention. They perform preventative checkups, which are part of a routine that gives patients ways to maintain and improve their health through smart eating choices, regular exercise, healthier lifestyle regimes, and regular checkups. While it is said that it's better to ask forgiveness after the fact, this is not one of those times.

As for the fear of death, dying can become a great fear for many, on so many levels. There's the fear of dying alone. There's the fear of dying too early. This fear can specifically become even more prominent when coupled with the anxiety of not having a significant impact upon society - the fear that we will die unknown, leaving no mark on the world, dying unloved without any memorable connection to the world around us, such as leaving a great work of art, a best-selling book, a unique piece of architecture, a charitable foundation, or a beautiful child to carry on the legacy of our name and memory.

There is a flip side to this. Losing someone you love can also cause one fear as well. But for either of these fears, the best remedy is to live your life as fully as possible, every moment of every day. Wallowing in self-pity does nothing for you. It only causes loss of time - which you'll never regain. Instead of placing blame and feeling sorry for oneself before it's too late, begin to look for the jewels in life, like the people who surround us. Cherish the little moments of pleasure, like reading on a rainy day, playing cards with friends, enjoying a meal together, talking, going for a walk, riding a bike, or a nice drive in the sun. Spend more time with your children. Make a conscious effort to sit down to dinner together on a regular basis and talk - without texting or watching TV, but talking with one another.

What's your biggest limitation? When thinking in terms of obstacles, what is keeping you from moving forward with your dreams and goals? Really, it's you. The truth of the matter is that no one puts limitations on you but yourself.

To really stretch yourself and build new muscles, it helps to identify what holds you back from trying new things. What keeps you from stepping out of your comfort zone?

Familiarity is one reason people choose not to change. I don't want to regress too much, but when I was very young, I had an abusive relative who pushed me around. I remained in that situation far too long because I didn't know any better at the time, and it was - for lack of a better reason - familiar. I was being paid attention to. In hindsight this rationale was very wrong, but at the time, being so young, I just didn't know any differently.

But now I do. And I'm assuming that since you are reading this book, that you, too, know the difference and want to see change for the better within your own life. So to that end, you may have to break the familiarity pattern.

Another reason people don't make a change is that they feel incapable. They feel they're not as gifted, talented, or as smart as others. And to that end, the only way to become capable and competent is to make the effort.

One thing that keeps people from stepping out of their comfort zones and taking on new challenges and risks is that they're waiting until just the right moment. The PERFECT time. And for most, that will never come.

Why?

Because until you are willing to take the first steps and make a few mistakes along the way, you are never going to get to perfection. Olympic medalist Michael Phelps did not start out winning. Princess Diana didn't start out as a princess. At one point, Mother Teresa and Mahatma Gandhi were just Sister Teresa and Mohandas.

The best phrase I know to get you to start anything NEW is **"Progress, not perfection."** Which means that unless you begin, you'll never have the chance to become truly great at anything.

So how far are you on the script you're writing? Have you opened the doors to your new business yet? Is that web site completed? Have you called any galleries to submit your paintings? Do you have your plane and hotel tickets yet for that amazing trip? Have you started walking in the morning to get fit yet? Start now. Not when you have just the "right" shoes, or the best business plan. Start NOW.

Recognizing A Good Break

"I haven't failed. I've just found 10,000 ways that don't work."

- Thomas Alva Edison on inventing the light bulb

You may be reading this book because you really want to make a change for yourself, or you might be someone who has simpler, more personal goals, like paying off your mortgage or organizing the house. Recognizing a good break is more about developing habits that become ingrained within you so things are easier for you to accomplish. It's about being open to the opportunities in your life.

Why is it that some people succeed in reaching their goals? Is it because they think they can? Attila the Hun didn't wait until the perfect moment when the cosmos were aligned and the settings were optimal. Lewis and Clark knew there would be perils and obstacles unknown and unforeseen. Lincoln didn't wait until he knew he wouldn't fail. In fact, he failed repeatedly. It wasn't until his fifties that he became President. So why did they all keep trying? Sometimes against great odds? The better question is why didn't they stop trying?

Actually, if you think about it, they didn't try. They just did it, and proceeded forward not knowing what the final outcome would be. All of these people had within them the ability to quit at any time and go do something less challenging, less confronting. Yet they chose the path with the greatest resistance. What was it that possessed them to do so? Truly, I think they saw within themselves, no other options. This was what they were determined to do. What they were destined to do. You might be saying, "But this isn't me... I'm not someone who is so bold or adventurous."

Not everyone needs to be so daring. You just need to be open to the idea of becoming someone who can reach their goals. But the lesson for all of us is not in how great the challenge or adventure is, but in the determination to get there. Even if your goal seems less lofty - like having financial security, finding a better job, or learning a new skill or trade - the methods are still the same. And the attitude remains the same. You will still need to have an objective and a desire. You'll need to make a decision within yourself that you truly want a change. And then you'll need to take action.

Top 1% Tip: This successful CEO of a major movie studio who touts the 2nd largest box office numbers, began his career as a gopher for a Producer after majoring in business and communications. From there he went from concert promoter to become a successful talent manager, to producing hit television shows. It was his ability to creatively spot talent and his prowess at meaningful *networking* that brought the success he enjoys today.

When I created the *Reach Now Institute,* I didn't know what the result would be. I didn't know how big it would become or how powerful an impact it would have. I just knew that this is what I had to do. I did have a direction and a focus. But I didn't know how I'd get there, however, I knew there were no other options for me. And I did hit some pretty major walls. Finances ran out. Interview sessions didn't get recorded. I had Internet problems, employee issues, and my mother at the time was sick with cancer and I was taking care of her in addition to building this company. So what drove me? I'm not sure what that inner passion was or where it came from, but I knew I had to go after it at all costs. I also knew that others before me in the business had succeeded so I knew it was possible. I also had enough *limitless* beliefs and enough successes under my belt through my own experiences, to know I was up for the challenge. What I didn't know at the time was just how challenging it was ultimately going to be.

I knew that I wanted to contribute to the world on a larger scale than I had before, and as I spoke with people about my ideas on how to accomplish this, I found that many were in need. They were looking for the roadmaps to success that I was creating.

Two things kept me driven; passion and a desire to fulfill my dream. I could really see myself ten and twenty years from now doing what I'm doing now because I'd created such a belief system within myself that there was no way it wouldn't turn out great. I visualized how this would look, how much I would impact the lives of others with my teachings, and how amazing my own life would be. What I didn't know was how I would get there or its level of success. I just knew that there was a destination and that I would find a way to get there.

This also didn't mean that I shouldn't have a game plan, an objective, and the ability to create a strategy to make this all happen. I still needed to outline and create a structure in which to accomplish my objectives by looking at what steps were necessary to get there and to keep moving forward to the next step.

Another thing I had to learn was to have several different options to get there. You don't want to have one path towards reaching your goal, because if that doesn't work, you hit a dead end. Instead, you want to have several options, in case one road is not working. The other thing that can benefit you is to have road markers along the way to help you gauge your progress or let you know if you're on the wrong path. For example, if you're starting an Internet business, one of your road markers can be deciding how many customers you want to have within a certain time frame, who your customers are, and how to find them. If you do achieve that goal, it becomes a great indicator to see what you did right or if not, how you need to change your strategies. You may decide before you reach a certain level of success that you'll use that road marker to strategize what your next step should be.

Always plan for every incident, whether it's a success or failure. It's just as important to have a plan for when you do succeed.

Sparking The Creative Seed

"Go confidently in the direction of your dreams. Live the life you have imagined."

    - Henry David Thoreau

If you're reading a book like this, I doubt it's because you're lacking in creativity. Instead, you simply may not have the time, energy, or an idea of how to begin your project or how to get it out of your head. You may have challenges with how to best access your creativity, and more importantly, how to cultivate it. There's a fallacy that if you aren't born with creativity that you'll never posses it. Creativity can and always has been cultivated in the right supportive environment. It's up to you to recognize what that right environment is for you and how to surround yourself with it.

One of the keys to creativity is to get out of your box. According to John C. Maxwell, finding new paradigms to expose yourself to is a very effective way to get out of your box. He suggests traveling abroad as one way to achieve this. On a simpler level, try a new venue for coffee. Go to a new or different neighborhood for lunch or dinner. Take up a new hobby. Do volunteer work. Not only are these great ways to stretch and challenge yourself, but they are excellent vehicles for sparking your creativity and can really get your juices flowing. When you open yourself up to new experiences, you allow your mind to see things in a new way. These are the seeds for building creative thoughts.

Why is creativity so easy for some? First let's address this by looking at where creativity comes from. It comes from inside your head, from within your mind. More to the point, it comes from your imagination. And what allows you to expand your imagination and fire up those creative synapses? Having no fear. Creativity is one of those unique little creatures that grows and is nurtured in a completely safe environment: your head. Your imagination allows you a safe place to take all the risks you wish and to be as bold and daring as you choose; because that creative idea of yours is in the safest of places and is nurtured to expand well beyond your limitations. We all have this ability within us. You just need practice to unleash it.

As a young boy I spent hours upon hours in treetops pretending I was Batman or Spider-Man and that a little piece of string in my hand was my spider webbing. And I also had an old spoon tied to the end of a long, worn piece of yarn that became my batarang. A young boy full of imagination, I was fearless, tough, and amazing within my imaginary world. Growing up poor, one can really get creative with yarn, colorful pajama bottoms, and an old piece of used cloth my mother made for me with the eye-holes cut out which became my costume of choice. The spoon became my weapon of choice - to help protect all of mankind and save the world from destruction. How cool is that?

So this begs a new question: What is the difference between imagination and creativity? I wasn't sure myself, so I looked them up. Imagination is the act or power of forming a mental image of something not present to the senses or never before wholly perceived in reality. It's the ability to form something from nothing, like the Internet, or a suspension bridge spanning two masses of land. Or a device to heat and prepare food faster. Creativity is having the quality of something created rather than imitated. The ability to make a new idea into a reality.

Both are pretty powerful. When Gene Roddenberry created *Star Trek,* he imagined a universe and beyond where people from different worlds, different ways of life, and unusual all coexisted. He saw a world and a time when doors opened automatically, and people were transported to other places through the dispersing of their molecules. A world and a time where breaking the sound barrier all the way to what he called warp speed was a common everyday occurrence. Where the boundaries of race and culture were no longer an issue. Where scanners were used to diagnose and treat people with diseases. Where ear pieces with no wires were used for communication. Where computer hard drives were small, fast, and powerful, containing massive amounts of data, processing them at lightening speeds. Where voice command was a standard way of communicating with machines. Where video and typed messages could be sent over light years with the click of a button. Where images are viewed on a flat, large screen.

Mr. Roddenberry had a great imagination. He put no limits or constraints on what could be done. He gave no thought to how it would be done. He just imagined that it was so.

Other creative people have found ways to make many of these wonderful things from Mr. Roddenberry's imagination become reality. We now send videos and typed communications over the Internet in a split second. (Some of us even get impatient when it doesn't happen fast enough!) Doctors now have portable scanners that can actually diagnose a person's vital signs. We now drive vehicles that we can actually give verbal commands to. Some can even self park! Many homes now have a large, flat plasma or LCD television from which they watch entertainment and surf the Internet. Some homes have voice command controlled heating and lighting functions. We use

Bluetooth technology to communicate and transfer data, and for wireless ear pieces so we can talk on the phone. Many people today have a small "backup" hard drive almost the size of a wallet to store several gigabytes of valuable information on. And I'm hard pressed these days to find a store that doesn't have automated sliding doors which open and close upon my presence, just like on the Enterprise.

Of the two, I wonder which is harder to do. To imagine the impossible, or to make the impossible a reality? And we do it all the time without even being aware of it. It's so common that there's even a phrase for it. When you use something meant for another purpose to do another function it wasn't originally meant for, we call that MacGyvering it. Have you ever used a credit card to unlatch or open a door? Or a coat hanger to get into a locked car? Maybe you've fashioned a shoelace to keep your necklace together. Or safety pinned a broach. Or used sugar packets to balance a table.

I'm not suggesting that you make a bomb out of cereal, old socks, and chewing tobacco, but in a pinch we all get creative and make things that were meant for one purpose take on an entirely new and different function. We do it with duct tape all the time; torn car seats, holding a broken bumper onto your car, keeping the broken door on the furnace closed, repairing a rip in your jeans or a torn bottom of a shoe in a pinch. We've jimmied, rigged, patched, propped, held, supported, or lifted things by MacGyvering them with an object or device designed to be used for another purpose.

I'm sure you've seen other people create something new from unusual items. Again, using safety pins, I've seen women's jewelry made more fashionable, and more expensive. I've seen purses made from hubcaps, and from seatbelts. Tennis shoes that light up. Greeting cards that sing. A five-blade razor for shaving! Instant hand warmers and a cell phone that connects to the Internet. Okay, maybe some devices should just stay with what they are and be a phone when I need it to be. Sorry, I digress, and that's an entirely different book.

My point is that imagination and creativity can come in all shapes and all sizes. So the real question now becomes what to do with them and how to get your thoughts and ideas to become a reality? As for having the time and freedom to do these creative things, let me ask you this: If you really did have the time, would you use it wisely?

Often when I hear people say they don't have time available in their busy schedules, the first thing I do is to give an exercise to determine if this really is true. More often than not, it turns out not to be as bad as they've suggested.

Have you ever had someone scrutinize your financial budget? In the beginning they ask you to keep a daily journal of every dollar and cent you spend each day. By the end of a week or two, you're able to see where your money is going and now you're able to change your patterns to become more fiscally fit and have the ability to save more.

I've used this same technique for time-management, and often by the end of the week my clients find that they had more free time available to them than they had realized.

Not every day is going to be the same, but at the end of the week I guarantee that you will have more free time than you originally thought.

I've also found that successful people seem to have no trouble making time for their goals and objectives. Now before you even say to me that it's because they have the money available to take the time, let me assure you that these habits of theirs are what created the successes and financial freedoms they have today, not the other way around.

In fact, I've found that many of them find creative ways to create even more time. They run or jog early in the morning, journal for 30 minutes to an hour or more every day, and still have alone time for the creative process. They even maximize their travel time by making phone calls (hands-free, of course), or listening to educational CDs.

—— FINISH LINE EXERCISE *1 of 2* ——

This one is **FUN**, but also **IMPORTANT**. You need to stretch your mind and your creative process.

List 10 things that would be classified as MacGyvering - just for the fun of it! Get your brain working here. This is where creativity and imagination can really expand and grow. i.e. You burned dinner. You have 8 people coming over in 40 minutes and all you have left is bread, eggs, onions, garlic, granulated sugar, dry pasta, salt, pepper, and a can of mushroom soup. What can you make?

HINT: You can turn granulated sugar into powdered sugar using an electric coffee grinder or a blender.

1.   6.

2.   7.

3.   8.

4.   9.

5.   10.

▶ **Create your MacGyver recipe**

(Using the ingredients listed at the top of the page):

1.

2.

3.

4.

5.

—— FINISH LINE EXERCISE *1 of 2 continued* ——

TIP: Don't get stuck in dinner mode. It's your choice whether you make breakfast, lunch or dinner for your guests.

For some this may seem like a silly exercise and one you might pass on. But the reason why goal reaching is hard for so many is that they are constricted by their ideas. This is the perfect opportunity to challenge yourself, to dance in your underwear, if you will.

Often we get locked into a set pattern of habits that we can't seem to get beyond which create limitations for us. The top people who distinguish themselves are those who are willing to look at things in a new way, and think differently than the pack mentality. Leaders are the ones who find a unique new path that ultimately leads to the finish line.

—— FINISH LINE EXERCISE *2 of 2* ——

Get yourself a little $1 notebook or pad and for one entire week track every minute you spend.

▶ Mark what time you took a shower or bath and how long it took.

▶ What time and how long did it take to do your makeup or to shave?

▶ Write down what time you prepared breakfast.

▶ What time you ate, and for how long?

▶ What time you washed the dishes.

▶ How long was your drive to work?

Make a tracking list like the example shown below. Keep track of everything that takes your time:

(Example)

Day: _____ Date: _____

Task: _____

Start Time: _____ Finish Time: _____

TIP: Add up your time each day. It's more likely than not that you find you have much more time available to you than you realized. If this is not the case, you will need to examine and reprioritize how constructively you are using your time every day.

—— FINISH LINE EXERCISE *2 of 2 continued* ——

CLUE: Here are some real time wasters –

▶ Texting or talking while driving or working on other projects (slows you down)

▶ Handling your email the day or the second it arrives (you can get this routine down to 2-3 times a week. REMEMBER: Most email sent to you is a request from someone else)

▶ Not preparing for the next day: making a list of projects the night before can save you on both mental and physical time that is valuable to you.

Exercise: Think of 5 things that are also time wasters and how you can maximize them making them more useful to you.

Your First Gift - Power Principle #1

"By appreciation, we make excellence in others our own property."

   - Voltaire

As promised, I'm letting you in on *Power Principle number One* early to illustrate how easy this program is going to be for you to master.

So what's a POWER PRINCIPLE?

A *Power Principle* is something that puts you in the right frame of mind and state, where the objective is to get you to finish what you start. I created these Principles to work together, so that they effectively build a pattern of positive habits within you.

What is *Power Principle number One*?

Power Principle number One is Build A Group.

Now why do you want to build a group, what will this group do for you, and how will it benefit you? The reason you want to build a group is that you're going to be creating what I call a CORE of people who will act as your foundation and your support.

So, what is CORE? CORE stands for Cooperation, Optimism, Reinforcement, and Empowerment. We'll get deeper into this later in the book so you can begin to understand how it works. The purpose of this group will be to get constant feedback and reinforcement from them.

Have you ever had someone give you a compliment you may not have been expecting -maybe on your hair, clothing, or how great you seem to be that day? Do you remember how that made you feel? We're going to take these same elements and magnify them adding some maximizing tools to give you encouragement, energy, and drive.

Here are the basic ideas behind *Power Principle number One*:

Your objective here is to put together a group of people whose purpose is to keep you motivated in your goals and help to keep you moving in a positive, forward direction until you achieve your desired outcome. Your group should consist of people who will act as your support, your clan or tribe, your unit, - your CORE. Your job will be to select people who will repeatedly give you positive, constructive feedback and be present. Also, as often as you can allow, personal interaction is a key element to creating a network of support.

If you're familiar with the concept of Mastermind groups, created by Napoleon Hill to give you the tools to become successful, then you'll immediately understand some of the concepts of this *Power Principle*. The difference here is that with a Mastermind group you must always meet with your group in person on a regular basis. Again, while this makes sense on so many levels and you can see positive results from this practice, it's impractical for many in today's climate of work and family obligations and general lack of time to keep this up for any sustainable length. So with that in mind, I've created something slightly different with many of the same added benefits including some new benefits to give you even greater momentum.

While Mastermind has done some amazing things and has created great results for many people over the years, it also takes a great deal of discipline to truly benefit from it. There are two inherent problems with a Mastermind group and I want to illustrate them so you can clearly see why and how I created *Power Principle One* to be a more effective and practical alternative.

While Mastermind meetings can take many forms, there are two basic types of Mastermind groups: one that is focused on the success and vision of one individual, and one that is focused on helping everyone in the group.

The second type of Mastermind group is one where all members of the group are meeting to support one another in achieving a goal. However, the practicality in addressing everyone's goals within that one sitting period can be difficult to manage. These types of groups are everywhere, even if they aren't always called Mastermind groups. An Alcoholics Anonymous meeting is a form of a Mastermind group, where the members get together to support each other in their sobriety, or coping with thereof. Although there are many other significant parts to mastermind groups which distinguish them entirely from 12-Step meetings.

Again, while there are incredible benefits to working with a Mastermind group, we are all aware that unless you have the time to meet regulary it can be difficult to get together on a consistent basis even for the most disciplined person.

Power Principle One focuses on working on one person at a time and thereby concentrates on using a two-person system instead of the larger group mentality. When you get together with more than two people, your mission often becomes less focused because everyone is waiting for their turn, and there is usually very little time for getting to each individual when it's their turn because time is limited and groups tend to take more time than often available. Groups are great for brainstorming, and there is something inherent in being in a room of creative, focused minds, but when you're trying to help each individual within the group, it's often not practical. However, it must be said that there is powerful inspiration and energy that can be gleaned from these larger meetings.

The second reason I chose to focus on a one-on-one format is that it's often harder to get more than two people together on a consistent schedule. It's why I also encourage you to get several people to be part of your CORE so when one person is not available, you're more likely to have others within your CORE who are more readily available to you. We all have busy, productive lives and cannot always be available for each other. Therefore the bigger your CORE, the more opportunities you'll have to find someone who is available to you.

Napoleon Hill, author of *Think and Grow Rich*, first defined the Mastermind group as a "coordination of knowledge and effort, in a spirit of harmony, between two or more people, for the attainment of a definite purpose." This thought is beautifully put.

As I've stated earlier, this concept is not something new. However, I've refined and hopefully improved on the idea to give you even greater momentum in achieving your goals. Another important distinction, as you'll soon see, is that this *Power Principle* does not work alone. It's only one element in the process of reaching your goals. I've created all *5 Power Principles* to work together. I've observed through my research that highly effective individuals continue to have consistent levels of achievement when using all *5 Power Principles*. They do not rely on only one method alone to reach their goals. This is an important key to their success.

Now I want to be very clear: Mr. Hill does say that creating a Mastermind group does not necessarily require fifty men, as Dale Carnegie used. Mastermind groups can be as small as two people and as big as one's ability to coordinate it. The primary distinction is the availability of everyone to meet on a regular, consistent basis.

To create a CORE that is dedicated to helping you achieve your personal goals, you can simply reach out to people in your network and explain to them that you are seeking their help and advice. Look for people who are like-minded or on a similar path, or who are slightly ahead of you in reaching their own objectives. You may be surprised at how willing people are to help, since it's an honor to be asked for one's advice or opinion.

You need not always meet with members of your CORE in person. You may find it easier sometimes to talk on the phone. However, I don't recommend always meeting this way. There are many more benefits you'll begin to understand through meeting in person.

When you are engaging with someone in person, their presence and energy can be important key factors in intensifying positive moments. Their presence plays an important part in your interaction.

Also, since a great number of us are more visual in how we take in our surroundings, when you get together with people you're usually some place where you're surrounded by sound, light, atmosphere, wind, music, the sun, the smell of food, or other stimuli that can heighten your awareness and make you even more present.

When you're put in a higher state, under these conditions, the impact of the meeting is more likely to stay with you than when you're just alone at home talking on the phone. Both are effective, but one has a better chance at learning a lasting impact.

Interaction is key. You don't want to isolate yourself too much, or you will lose the momentum of that positive feeling and feedback you receive.

People who spend too much time at home alone often experience several negative side effects. They tend to procrastinate more and find other things to do instead of specifically what's on their goal list. They tend to straighten up the house or find errands or projects that suddenly become more important than meeting their objectives. A person can also get easily sad and way too contemplative when spending too much time home alone. There's a tendency to become more reflective in a negative way and second-guess or judge themselves too harshly. Has that ever happened to you?

Here are some of the characteristics of the *SELF* paradigm:

Too Much Inner Thought: Not stepping outside of the circle can keep you stuck

Constant Self Reflection: This can often turn into self criticism

Greater Time Spent In Isolation: You may lose energy, drive, and focus

Non-Productive Inward Objectivity: Second guessing yourself will stall your progress

You'll want to opt to get out and meet the people in your CORE in person. Shake up your routine. Get out of your complacency as much as possible.

What are some quality traits of highly successful people?

In researching the lives of successful, thriving, happy people who live their lives to the fullest, I found some recurring themes in their relationships with people.

The themes are usually in one of four areas:

- Some of them came from a strong, healthy family background. (Notice I use the word healthy.)

- Others have a solid, loving, supportive marriage, where they and their spouse communicate and listen to each other and give value and encouragement.

- A third group are those that developed strong ties with friends in college who they're still close to - people they spent many hours working, studying, and playing together with.

- The forth group developed a very supportive, highly constructive involvement with business associates, who all remain close and tight-knit.

What do these four groups have in common? They all have a good foundation of support in their lives.

Does it mean that they rely on other people to rescue them or carry them through their task? No. What is does mean is that the people in their lives give them support and encouragement that helps to instill in them the confidence that they can accomplish *anything* they put their minds to. The support they receive comes in the form of encouragement and positive feedback.

So how do they do this?

Have you ever met someone who came from a strong, supportive family? Of course you have. And what do you notice immediately about them? Well, the first thing you might notice is that they're someone who enjoys life and really sees the blessings and good things in life.

What are some of their positive qualities?

These people are usually open to new experiences, they have a relaxed, laid back -almost like they're in control - attitude, and they're up for any adventure.

What's another thing that helps to identify them?

The next thing you might notice about them is that they like people. They are genuinely interested in all of the people around them, and they really value what those people have to say. They want to get to meet and know as many new and different people as possible, because they understand how much it enriches and adds value to their own lives.

What's the benefit for this outgoing type of personality?

You can instantly see how curious and interested they are in their surroundings. They take in everything from the weather to the trees, the architecture of an old building, and the way others talk and interact. Everything from smell, sight, sound, feelings, and taste are all always new and exciting to them - like mini adventures. And they're extremely curious. They're always questioning, very appreciative, and genuinely interested to learn more. And they all exude confidence.

How did they do this?

By having good, supportive role models, (which we'll talk about later), that instill the tools of confidence to be able to go out into the world with love knowing that even if they fail it's not the end of the world.

This is an important distinction; when someone fails who is not the problem, what do they do? They readjust their methods and continue to move forward until they achieve the desired effect.

Said in a different way: when someone who is confident and competent fails, they don't quit. They reexamine their situation, look at all the angles, and come to terms with what may have lead to their lack of success. Then they push forward from a *new* direction until they successfully achieve their desired outcome.

Top 1% Tip: This head of a major studio meets regularly at his house with friends and associates on a strictly social basis. He has always been genuinely interested in being with and around these people, and gets lots of benefits from every encounter. As a result of his genuine and sincere interest in others, they often recommend him to their coveted, successful associates.

What if you don't posses any of these qualities? This is where *Power Principle One* comes into play. Everyone has at least one person they call a friend. For example, take students who are in law school or medical school. They spend hours upon hours studying and working together, and when they do their first year as an intern at a hospital or their first year at a law firm where they're required to bill hundreds and hundreds of hours, they build an even greater bond with their peers than they did in school. They support and encourage and push each other to make it through, because they all know that if they can just get through the first grueling year, they'll have the physical and mental discipline to continue on.

Their school friends who're now work associates encourage and support them to keep moving forward. They network and share resources with each other. Ultimately, they get the end results they desire.

As Malcolm Gladwell noted in his book Outliers *(Outliers: why do some people succeed, living remarkably productive and impactful lives, while so many more never reach their potential?)*, you can look at Bill Gates or Steve Jobs if you want an example of business associates. Along with people like Paul Allen, Steve Wozniak and others who spent thousands of hours together writing code, learning and training themselves, and building the foundations for their successes.

During this time, when they were tired, frustrated, and sometimes hungry, they supported and encouraged each other to push forward because they all knew that each one of them had within them the power to make their dreams a reality.

How do you find this kind of support for you? Well, you may be surprised to learn that you may already have a similar kind of support now. Again, all of us have at least one friend we talk with on a regular basis, right?

There are two things at play here. When you think about calling this person, why do you typically call them? Sure, it might be because you were thinking about the person and wanted to see how they're doing. Usually there's a secondary reason. But if you really think about it, it's because you want to catch the other person up on what you're doing and get their constructive feedback. And then, what else happens? They usually will give you support and encouragement and acknowledge that what you're doing is great or on the right track.

For example, you may call someone and tell them what's going on in your life. They listen, encourage you, maybe offer you some reflection or direction, and give you kudos for what you're doing. If that sounds contrived to you, think about a recent phone call or meeting you've had with a friend.

Ask yourself these questions:

1. Who called whom?

2. Why?

3. What did you talk about?

4. What was their response?

5. Did you feel good about the call?

6. What emotions did it bring up for you?

7. Did it improve your energy level?

8. Did your attitude change for the better?

Take a moment and think about how you responded.

Does this make sense to you? Perhaps you recalled a recent conversation or phone call that wasn't pleasant. Think about why. Did you or your friend use that time to emotionally dump onto the conversation? I'm not suggesting that there won't be times when you need to commiserate, but that's not the point or reason behind these sessions. Remember, your goal here is to get helpful, constructive feedback that encourages you to move forward.

Perhaps you were talking with a family member. I don't always recommend family members for this kind of feedback, since a lot of us didn't come from the most supportive of families, and while they may be doing their best to support us, it often takes the form of criticism or expressed in a way that pretty much can burst your hope bubble. Sometimes with the best of intentions it can come out sounding unsupportive.

When you call someone in your CORE, they'll listen to you and give real kudos and support. When you hang up, you're feeling pretty good about yourself and you want to take the momentum of that feeling and continue what you're doing even more! And this will occur naturally.

That's the power of connection.

And when you have more than one person to do this within your CORE - since not everyone will be available when you need them to be - it can be a pretty powerful motivator to help you stay on the right track and keep moving forward.

It's the essence of *Power Principle One*: Having a solid, supportive, team, unit, family, or CORE.

Again, CORE stands for:

Cooperation — Work together as a team. Support one another to feel energized, motivated, and empowered, to keep everyone on the right path.

Optimism — Supporting the people in your CORE with encouragement strengthens everyone. Positive, constructive, support and feedback are the keys to reaching your goals.

Reinforcement — Acknowledging and recognizing each other's progress builds strong foundations of accomplishment.

Empowerment — Encouragement is a powerful motivator to strengthen one's desire to fulfill their objectives. This is an important tool for staying on the right track.

These are the four elements you want to look for when you're building your group.

If you can put this into place or if you can strengthen the CORE you already have, it can be a huge factor in your movement towards achieving your goals.

When you have several people encouraging and pushing you forward, you get this incredible sense of accomplishment, and that positive energy keeps you moving.

Here are some of the benefits of being part of an effective group:

- Increased Creativity
- Greater Spirituality
- A Supportive and Loving Environment
- Healthy Social Outlet
- Constructive Feedback and Support
- Greater Mental, Spiritual, and Physical Energy
- Fun, Laughter, Fulfillment
- Commonality with Like-Minded People
- Heightened Outward Expression and Personality

Now, does following *Power Principle One* carry you through to completion? Not alone. But, it's a great first step towards getting to where you want. Remember, this is just the first of the *5 Power Principles*, and combining them together is what gives you that maximum energy and drive.

Think of it this way: Even the simplest of compliments can change your state dramatically. But when a peer who really knows you and understands you gives you positive reinforcement, you feel like you can do anything.

Why do we have friends? For support, value in our lives, fun, and commiseration. And we usually choose someone who is at our level or slightly above us. Can you think of a reason why that is? To keep us climbing and moving forward. We share our deepest thoughts and emotions with this person because this is someone we value and trust them to be there for us.

As you get better at *Power Principle One* and you have more and more successes with your CORE, then when you do have those alone times, they're going to work in your favor and become more effective for you. You'll actually feel more empowered. Eventually, *alone* won't make you lose momentum. You'll maximize your time and energy towards getting things accomplished.

Warning: Don't use the time you spend with your CORE as a time to dump and pour out your emotions. There's a time and place when you can do this. The focus of these sessions is to share your progress and get constructive feedback.

If you use these times together only to dwell in misery or wallow in negative conversations, you're likely to accomplish two things: First, you'll bring the other person down and waste a lot of time and energy emotionally sapping the mood from both of you. Second, if you do this too much, I can guarantee your friends are not going to have time for you. It is emotionally draining to listen to another person's problems all the time.

I'm not saying that there won't be times when you will need a friend's ear or a shoulder to cry on because you've lost a loved one, your marriage or relationship is rocky, you got laid off from work, or you just had a bad day. I know all of these things are part of life and there is a time when you'll need the help and counsel of a friend. There is a time and place for everything. Ultimately you want to continue to move forward towards reaching your goals.

Support is a two-way street. In Power Principle #2 you're going to learn how to get even more energy and drive by helping others in your group. Keep in mind that while you are accumulating more tools as you continue to read on, you are also building a formula for yourself that is going to take you even closer towards reaching your goals.

—— FINISH LINE EXERCISE ——

▶ What type of people motivate you?

▶ What is it about them that attracts you to them?

▶ Is it their drive and energy?

▶ Is it in their passion for life or is it found in how they pursue their goal?

▶ Is it something specifically about the field they work in?

▶ Is it something you observe about the way they live life fully?

▶ Or perhaps it's in your admiration of the possessions they own.

In this exercise, find five things about someone that motivates you through their drive for life. Chose someone who's life you might desire for yourself.

Write these five things down on a piece of paper, leaving enough room by each one, and write for three minutes (per item) how you too might incorporate these same qualities into your own life.

Then take a moment to think about how you can put all five of these things together and apply them successfully to improve the quality of your own life.

▶ Who motivates you?:

—— FINISH LINE EXERCISE *continued* ——

► What specific qualities do you admire?

1.

2.

3.

4.

5.

► How can you use these tools they possess in your own life?

TIP: Make sure you write about someone's qualities and not about possessions they have that you desire. When you are successful you can acquire possessions. What we're looking for here are the qualities that make you successful.

Overcoming A Limiting Mindset

"Twenty years from now you will be more disappointed by the things you didn't do than the ones you did do. Explore. Dream."

　- Mark Twain

Self-help is fundamentally a good thing. Its very nature is to help you grow, expand, and become a better, more satisfying you. It provides processes to assist you in growing and reaching goals.

But there is an inherent problem built into self-help - one that has rarely been acknowledged in the past, but that's getting more recognition every day.

Here's the funny thing about Self-help; the word *Self* is ironically the problem with Self-help. The majority of people who go after any type of Self-help program will often fail. The exceptions are the rare few who can go at it alone successfully.

Self-help by its very nature seems doomed to failure. Why? When something so profound in its awareness is supposed to elevate you and give you clarity, it seems ironic that oftentimes self-help is the very thing that can put you right back to where you started. The double edged sword here is if this was purposely set up this way by the powers that be so you will be forced to buy more self-help materials.

Typically, when most people go to the gym, or they decide to lose weight through a program like Weight Watchers or Jenny Craig, they set off to do these things *alone*. Think about how many home self-improvement courses you've purchased. Now consider how many of them you saw through to completion, and how many are now sitting on the shelf, tucked into the back of a closet, stuffed in the garage, or laying under your bed collecting dust.

Why is this? We start off with the highest ambition, driven by the best of intentions to see it through to completion. We were really looking forward to making great strides and changes. But ultimately, doing it alone quickly became boring and unsatisfying.

Now I'm not saying to never be alone, and I'm not suggesting that if you don't find people right now to do stuff with you're a loser and not worthy of anything. That's not what I'm saying at all. I'm also not suggesting that there aren't people who can do things well on their own. There are. And of course they can. You may be someone who regularly goes to the gym alone and are very productive and satisfied with your routine. As I stated earlier, there are people who come from strong, supportive relationships where they've already built a solid sense of *self* through the dynamic of a group energy that reinforces and encourages them.

So what is the difference between people who successfully do things on their own and people who struggle and lose momentum? If you're someone who goes to the gym regularly on your own, you may view that time as a reward away from our family or work obligations. Private time can be very healthy. And you may benefit from this alone time because you come from a strong supportive background and you're confident being on your own.

What I'm suggesting here is that having the moral support and encouragement of others on a consistent basis can do wonders for you. It can give you added energy when you need it most to carry you through to your goals. And you want to always look for ways to get more energy and drive out of everything you do. Let's face it, doing anything for a sustained duration of time alone can become boring and lose its enticement.

Working towards a goal can be exciting in the beginning. But for some, the novelty can eventually wear out, and you can easily and very rapidly become bored and unsatisfied. Think of it this way: If you went to dinner, the movies, an art exhibit, or even a vacation alone all the time, in the beginning you might be ok with it, but eventually you're going to lose your passion for what you're doing.

Is it ok to be alone? Yes. In fact, there are times we relish our down time, our alone time. It can calm and center us. Can you feel great being alone? Again, the answer is yes. In fact, I'm going to show you how when you incorporate the 5 *Power Principles* into your life you are going to have so much energy and drive that you are going to really value and look forward to your alone time. You'll feel more empowered, more full of life and more excited about everything you do. You're no longer going to see being alone in a negative light but as an added bonus to your life. It's strange to think that using the power of others is going to make you a stronger self. But it's true, and the benefits are huge.

Success and progress is a constantly moving target. Whenever we make progress in our lives or reach a goal, we create newer or bigger ones for ourselves. So I'm not suggesting that the lessons in this book will make you never want to strive and challenge yourself again, or that you will reach the ultimate peak and never push yourself again. On the contrary, this book was created to help you reach those higher peaks that seemed out of your grasp. The ones that in the past seemed unattainable. The ones that somehow you stopped striving for. You're going to be able to push past the ceiling that was once there. Success should be ever evolving and constantly changing, because this is the key to the circle of life.

You may become dissatisfied with your present job and want to work for yourself or do something different. You may be restless and unsettled about never having enough time to travel, and you want to start taking more vacations and exploring the world. You may be tired of how your house looks and you're ready for a dramatic home makeover. Or you might already be playing at a very high level in your life and career, but you can't seem to break through the ceiling that would allow you to enjoy life at an even greater level than ever before.

Whatever your reasons are for reading this book, my goal is to give you the tools to accomplish your goals by showing you hidden treasures that successful people do which makes them successful. Throughout the book you'll notice that we're using examples of those top people who are the most successful in the world, how they got there and what keeps them constantly climbing and striving. You too should be able to enjoy the rewards of success, and it's within your power to achieve them.

Again, sitting on the sidelines and reading a book on improvement or motivation is not going to do the trick. You must take action. But what is the difference between this and all the other books you've read?

Any book on improving your life is intentionally good and meant only to help you to succeed. However, some of the steps to get you there can be overwhelming and difficult for you. While they often show you what to do, the methods of execution are different for everyone. In other words, you wouldn't try to lift 200 pounds of weight if it was your first time in the gym. You wouldn't sign up for a dance contest if you were just starting out. We are all at different stages in our progress. And, sometimes the steps a self-help author suggests you take may not be best for your current level.

I've designed this book and the exercises to work for everyone at any level. They're not hard to practice and not so intense as to make you put them aside after a while. In fact, they're so basic that you might be surprised to know that on some level you're already using a few of them in your life now.

I believe a primary reason why so many of us fail to accomplish our goals is because so often we try to do it alone. And while determination can be a great motivator for getting you revved up and started, it doesn't sustain your drive for very long.

The simple truth is that doing something alone for extended periods of time gets boring. There's no sustainable passion in doing something on your own. On the contrary, when you do something with others, you find that you have an increased drive, energy, passion, excitement, and power to get it done. You go after it with gusto and child-like enthusiasm. This is the essence of *Power Principle One.*

Every good self-improvement course or book actually touches on this theme, even though most authors never write more than a few paragraphs or a chapter or two about it. Amazing people like Stephen Covey, Tony Robbins, Brian Tracy, and Eben Pagan, Wayne Dyer, and others all touch upon it, even recognize it and address it. They all understand and see the importance and value in it. And it is valuable. Probably one of the most fundamentally important parts of what the successful people have in their lives that continues to keep them successful. Even business people understand the importance of the *group concept*. It's why they have regular group meetings. It's why so many people in my field speak at companies and corporations to motivate and drive these same people. And while it is the basis of productivity staying on the road to success, it is only one part of your overall success. Just like flour is to cake, having a strong group is just one ingredient you need towards your overall success. It may be the base, but you still need the other ingredients to create a really tasty dessert.

Think of this like a high performance vehicle. If a CORE of strong, sound relationships is the engine, then you still need brakes, tires, fuel, a proper steering wheel, a safety windshield and other components to make it functional and perform well. And to get your vehicle to perform at its peak and win the race, you still need to fine-tune it. You need to make sure the wheels are balanced and in good shape. You need to make sure the steering wheel is tight and does not move too much to the right or left. The windshield needs to be positioned and tilted just so to give it maximum aerodynamics. If you want the highest possible performance, you'll need to remove attachments on your car that can cause wind resistance and decrease aerodynamics. The brakes need to be sound. The fuel injection system needs to provide the right amount of fuel at the proper times. You'll also need a great pit crew, and so much more if you want to win the race. When you think about it, every part is equally important, because you're only as strong as your weakest part.

Understanding The Difference Between Self-help And Self-Improvement

"Two roads diverged in the woods, and I… I took the one less traveled by, and that has made all the difference."

- Robert Frost

When taking on any self-help practice, we're usually dealing with something that's an issue in our life we wish to change or to get rid of completely. We work on things that we're unsettled by. Something that bothers us, emotionally drains us, or is holding us back. Perhaps it's our weight, a tired career, a rocky relationship, our dwindling finances, or personal and family issues. Self-help teaches us to deal with issues that we want to overcome, that often overwhelm us and bring us to a lower place in our lives.

Often people who look to Self-help for answers feel like they're different from others, that they're not clued into life the way they see others are. Often, they feel less than other people, or separate and alone. They also wonder why other people seem to fit into society and why they themselves are always struggling to fit in.

But more often than not, the simple truth is, people are just lacking answers in their lives, and they aren't always sure where to go to find those answers. So they turn to Self-Help and other programs. Why? Simple; so they can fit in.

You want to hear an interesting irony about fitting in? You've heard of the Goth subculture, right? Goth kids typically dress in dark, often black clothing. They wear dark eye makeup and dark lipstick, and they wear their hair long in front so it usually covers their eyes. They rarely look at others and call themselves loners because they feel they're too different and don't fit into society. The character Violet from the movie *The Incredibles* was kind of like that.

Here's where it gets interesting: Goth kids feel they have been spurned and don't fit into "normal" society. They feel they're free thinkers. They do not accept the way "it is." And so they isolate themselves into an individual mentality. Then what happens? They band together and form... wait for it... groups! They get their sense of identity and sense of self from the group mentality. They assert their individuality through groups!

Here's another interesting factoid: They actually embody some of the very things that successful people do. Interesting, huh? They are free thinkers. They do not accept the way things are, and are constantly looking for a new or better way. And, they enjoy the company of other like-minded individuals.

Self-Improvement on the other hand, comes from the desire to learn a new skill, stretch ourselves, and work towards creating a better life for our self. When our goals are focused on Self-Improvement, it's partly because we are unsatisfied with our current situation not because we're unhappy, but more because we want even more for ourselves than what we presently have. When someone is focused on Self-Improvement they are looking to take their life to a greater, more powerful place. We see others who have something we too desire and think: Why not me? And we seek the information and best path in which to get there. We find the motivation, the drive, the desire to go after what we want - whether it's a better career, starting your own business, having financial freedom, finding that amazing relationship that makes your life full, or getting your body into incredible shape.

We All Want Change

"It is not the strongest of the species that survive, nor the most intelligent, but the one most responsive to change."

- Charles Darwin

Think about any Self-Improvement program you've been to, book you've read, CD, DVD, or tape you've listened to. In the beginning you were pumped and determined that this time you were going to make it work. This was the one. You've blown tons of cash on late-night infomercials that promise that this time you've found the magic bullet. So you opened your wallet, pulled out the credit card, and bought yet another item guaranteed to improve your life. And what did you do? First, you went back and forth about whether or not to pay for the rush shipping because you knew that this was the one. This thing was the end-all, be-all to finally make your life fantastic. So you told the operator, "Yes, I'd like rush shipping."

Then you waited and waited until the package arrived. You hoped that the packaging would be plain-wrapped so you don't have to endure the embarrassment of friends or neighbors seeing that home exercise kit, or weight loss program, complete with books, supplements, resistance bands, and an exercise mat. But by the time it arrived you rationalized that you didn't care what others thought, because this was about your improvement.

When it arrived you ripped into the box and fawned over all the materials. You looked at the pictures and read the words that promised to transform you into a god or goddess, or at least a better human being. You thought, This is it! This is the *golden ticket* I've been searching for my entire life. It's the thing that will make the difference, this time. No more feeling less than others, no more self-conscious thoughts, no more wondering what others think of you. Finally, you were going to be someone envied, respected, and admired.

So you jumped right in and began.

I remember when I got a program called P90X because I was sick of being out of shape. I was thirty pounds heavy, and I couldn't remember the last time I had been comfortable tucking my shirt in.

There were two things that really changed my attitude about wanting to get into shape and improve my physique. One of them was a photo of me taken at my own birthday party in Las Vegas. I was with some great friends and this beautiful woman I was seeing at the time. We were at a Japanese restaurant where everyone had taken me to celebrate my birthday and a photo was taken of me blowing out my birthday candles. The waiter who took the picture shot it from an angle that allowed him to get everyone on both sides of our table. But what he also captured was so dismaying to me that it caused a radical shift in my thinking. It changed how I saw myself for the first time. In the picture you could see my entire torso. I was wearing a gray T-shirt and my "love handles" were enormous. To me, these things were so large that I thought I looked like Jabba the Hutt in a gray shirt. I was mortified when I saw this picture. Here I was with this incredibly beautiful woman and I couldn't help wondering why she was with this enormously fat person. They say the camera adds ten pounds. Try thirty!

I was so devastated that I soon broke up with her. In retrospect, it was an irrational thing to do, but at the time it also felt very real for me. Since then we've become the closet of friends and still love and support each other to this day.

The second thing that caused this dramatic change in me was when I was on a trip to Hawaii. Here I was in this gorgeous, incredible paradise, in the bluest, blue-green, crystal-clear water you could ever imagine, and I was the only guy in the water with a shirt on! Can you imagine? Which ultimately didn't help my situation. Instead of hiding my more-displeasing features, the wet shirt clung to the unsightly parts of my body only to magnify the visual even more. From that day on, for the rest of the trip, I never went into the water except at night. I couldn't subject myself and other people to my out-of-shape body. The pain of remaining in my current situation was so great it caused a radical shift in my thinking.

So when the P90X package arrived, I tore into it with gusto. If you've ever used this program you know how serious and intense it is, and the results it can bring are amazing. I couldn't wait to begin. I went to my kitchen and threw out everything that was bad to eat. I ran to the store and got everything I needed to get a healthy body. I bought the necessary weights, mats, shoes, and chin-up bar needed to do the workout. And I put the first DVD into the player and began my journey to fitness. Every day for seven weeks I worked hard at attacking this 90-day program. And it was tough. For the first few weeks I could barely get through a session. But I kept at it. I was in that much discomfort about my current situation and I was determined to change. I committed time everyday to getting into shape. Nothing was going to stop me. I also changed my eating habits and improved my diet and eating schedule. I consciously ate slower, and I paid more attention to what I was consuming. And I did the exercises with drive. In the beginning, of course, it was difficult. I could barely do half a chin up while using a chair to support me! But eventually I was able to do more and more reps and complete the entire routine. And then, at week seven, something happened.

I started skipping days. I made excuses and rationalizations that life got in the way and I would get back on track tomorrow. Then another day went by, and another. I noticed that I was not having as much fun at this. My determination was slipping fast. My enthusiasm was waning and I wasn't as motivated. It didn't make sense. Here I was, in the best shape I'd ever been in my life! Not only could I tuck in my shirt, but I was also comfortable taking it off in public. I even had to buy new pants and jeans, two sizes smaller! This is what I was waiting for! So what changed?

It got boring. It lost its excitement for me. It felt alone. I wasn't feeling that incredible sensation I had when I first purchased the program. My enthusiasm left me. Was it a bad program? No. It was, in fact, a great program. And the results were very noticeable. So what was it? It was me. I was bored doing this alone. I was no longer revved up about finishing the entire ninety days. I was burnt out.

So my old eating habits soon returned. I laid on the couch and watched a lot of TV. I ate more unhealthy snacks and some of the weight returned. Was I a bad person? Was I someone who was just never going to be able to accomplish a goal like this? No. I was just a person like many others who began improving their situation alone and it wasn't enjoyable anymore.

Of course, there are always things we do alone and are very capable of doing, and we'll look at what sustains us in those times. The goal here is to get you through completion in whatever you do whether by yourself or with a group. We will continue to focus on ways to improve your success rate and keep you motivated through to the end.

By the end of this book you will have all the tools necessary to keep you motivated all the way to the *finish line*. Are you ready for the rest of the *Power Principles*? Throughout this book you've been given tons of exercises that actually incorporate each of the *Power Principles*. After you see what each one is in greater detail, we'll go even deeper into understanding how to successfully use them and integrate them seamlessly into your everyday life taking you to the next level of your success evolution.

Where Are You In Your Life Right Now?

"If you obey all the rules… you'll miss all the fun."

   - Katharine Hepburn

To make changes and to begin to see progress in our lives we have to understand where we are, which also gives us an understanding of where we want to go. So what are the indicators in your life that tell you where you are at the present moment in your life? I know you have some. At the end of every year, people make New Year's resolutions of things they will do to improve their lives. A new direction can mean making changes to rid yourself of things that weren't working before and choosing something better for yourself.

New Year's resolutions often come out of the need to rid ourselves of something that is causing great discomfort or pain in our lives. The problem with New Year's resolutions is that the majority of us never reach our resolutions. Then we're left with this lousy feeling that we're incapable of reaching our goals. And most people tend to beat themselves up emotionally over this.

After experiencing this problem again and again in my own life, I decided that I would no longer set myself up for failure. Instead, I'd put a regime into place that would make me accountable and give me a way to see progress that was making a difference in my life. I needed to see something that gave me real changes and improvement. So I created a task list. Another major problem with New Year's resolutions is that most of us keep them inside our heads, cluttered with all the other things in our busy lives that we have to manage and deal with on a daily basis. If we do it that way, sooner or later the resolution is going to get pushed aside or to the back of the line. And when we do finally remember it, we now feel bad and beat ourselves up because we didn't reach that goal.

So instead I created a list of things I would accomplish. I did this towards the years beginning instead of waiting until the end. I put a date on top, gave each one a specific project deadline, and posted it in several areas of my house so I'd be forced to see the written words every day, reminding me of my goals. I also added some mantras and affirmations that would get me in the proper frame of mind to go after my goals and meet the objectives I'd presented to myself.

What I Expect of Myself for 2009

What will it take to get to the next level?

- Keep my emotions in check. (Don't react immediately. Always get more info first)
- Show more interest in others. (Everyone has something to offer)
- Save more (put 10% of my income into savings or investments every week). Have $5,000 saved by October 2009
- Invest more (manage my investment portfolios and make sure they are growing)
- Pay off ALL debts by November 1st, 2009 (get rid of the biggest debts first to see real progress)
- Build relationships with my family (spend more quality time with my mom).
- Work harder (stretch myself to get beyond the fears and push through the tired)
- Learn and acquire new skills to grow my skill-set

- Be patient with people. (Don't offer my opinion unless asked for. Find their nuggets)
- Talk less, Listen more. (Be open to learning every day)
- EXERCISE Daily at 8am. (30 pounds in 3 months - December 2009)
- Cook more (Take cooking classes to expand my techniques). Sign up for 2 by July 1st
- Find new hobbies. (Take courses on speaking and putting seminars together) sign up for June
- Spend more time with friends. (If I die tomorrow, did I spend enough quality time?)
- Invest more in philanthropic and world ventures, charities & helping others
- Create my own philanthropic organization by July 2010

The key to every action is one little step forward every day. Excuses will arise every day; being tired, not in the mood, feeling overworked, or feeling sad. Push through them and think only about the goal.

Value everything you have. Cherish the little and big accomplishments.

Love the world even when it won't love you back. Your mission is not to be liked but to make a positive change.

DON'T JUST TALK THE TALK. DO IT!

Don't question or second-guess yourself. Everyone does that. Push forward. Make every one count.

Don't be afraid to stand up for yourself and your beliefs. Try not to be a people pleaser. That is not a good motivation for action.

Take greater and greater risks. Challenge yourself. Push the edges and make them hurt like growing pains. Don't stay in the comfort but enjoy the comfort at the end of every step.

Care about others. Love those you disdain the most. Find their qualities and encourage and support them.

Love yourself most of all.

While the goals changed as I accomplished each one, the mantras remained the same and I recited them out loud every day. I also checked off the goals I accomplished for even more impact and satisfaction once completed.

Progress is key here, not perfection. Don't get caught up in the perfection of a goal because it will keep you from mastering it. Just concentrate on practice and repetition. I highly recommend something like this for yourself to keep you motivated and accountable for reaching the objectives you set for yourself.

What Are You Searching For?

"Seek first to understand, then be understood."

    - Stephen Covey

Even though everyone is looking to improve something in their lives, our motivation for improving is always different for everyone. You may want to take some of the pain out of your life. You may be driven to accomplish what you see others have achieved, and you wonder how you too can get the same results for yourself. You may want to let go or get rid of the things in your life that have been holding you back and keeping you from reaching your dreams.

So what is it that you're looking for? Do you want to improve upon something in your life, or is it something new you want to take on? Perhaps it's a better home. Or to travel to new and exotic destinations. Perhaps you're someone who's looking to change careers, and you want to be more successful than you have in the past. And for some, it's to get rid of the things in your life that kept you mentally and emotionally from moving forward.

But you can't be in the middle of the road if you really want to see successful, dramatic change. Whatever it may be there are several things that need to occur in order to make that change effective. You must have either a great pain about the current situation you're in or you are so passionate about something in your life you want that nothing can sway or move you from having or achieving it.

Today is the day you dig deep and really take the time to find what you are most passionate about.

Commit to finding something that will elevate you to a new level of life. As humans we are most happy when we are growing. We grow most when we find new challenges that fulfill us and also improve our lives.

It's said that we are actually happiest in the pursuit of a goal then reaching the actual goal itself. Another way to say this is that the adventure is more fulfilling than the results.

Tapping into your passion is where you'll find fulfillment, adventure and growth.

Why Do You Have To Learn Something New?

"Personally, I'm always ready to learn, although I do not always like being taught."

- Sir Winston Churchill

You may be thinking to yourself about how you've just spent more money again on yet another program. Why is this one going to be any different than the others in the past? What is the magic bullet this time? When I wrote this book it was with those same questions in mind. I was frustrated and confused as to why people were spending so much time and money on programs they bought over and over again only to find themselves right back where they started. I couldn't get over the fact that only a few were succeeding, and the majority didn't seem to be making any progress. I kept asking why?

I developed this program and book as a way to shift the percentages. If eighty percent were failing and twenty percent were succeeding, why couldn't that formula be flipped around so that more people had successes and fewer people failed? There's plenty of room for more successful people in the world. It isn't like there's a cap on how many achievers are allowed in the world. So why did this backwards formula even exist?

Every Self-Help and Self-Improvement course and book that I used all had the right idea. All of them touched upon these problems, but they never took it any further. As I've mentioned throughout this book the main problem with any Self-help course is in the word "self". More often than not, doing things alone will eventually lead people to stop what they're doing because it becomes boring or "lonely". They lose their momentum and drive.

Again, although this is a primary reason why people don't complete their mission, it is just a small piece of the overall puzzle for success. It's just one of the 5 *Power Principles*.

So who are we as individuals? Or perhaps a better question is, how do we want others to perceive us? When we set goals for ourselves and we go after achievements, are we motivated by an inner drive to succeed or by the need to prove to others that we too are significant and have a place in the world?

Some people are driven to accomplish a task or reach a goal by the need to prove to someone else that they can do it, like their parents. On the surface this is not necessarily a bad motivation, but it can ultimately have some pitfalls and keep you from accomplishing your goals. Remember, real change comes from the need to get out of the pain of a current situation or from your passionate desire that you simply must make a change for the better.

If you're someone who came from a rough childhood, where your family was not as supportive as you would have liked, and you were often made to feel less than significant, you may be motivated to prove those negative attitudes about you were wrong. You may have a nagging inner voice inside your head that you want to prove wrong.

In the next section we're going to examine this "inner voice" deeper, and look at ways to keep this voice from continuing to hold you back. This process will give you a chance to even the playing field and allow you to focus on your objectives without additional roadblocks that would hinder your progress.

That Nagging Inner Voice

"The time to repair the roof is when the sun is shining."

- John F. Kennedy

If you really listen to that nagging inner voice, which is more negative than positive, you'll find that it's not your own. Because your own voice would not be making negative comments in the first place! Your authentic inner voice wants you to achieve and succeed in life. So the voice inside of you that continually berates and puts you down is not your true voice.

Where does this voice come from? Often it is the voice of a parent or sibling whose years of constant berating or negative feedback has triggered a roadblock within you, keeping you from progressing in your life in a smooth, productive manner. Later in life, it may show up as a non-supportive spouse who is too critical of you and offers nothing but negative opinions about how you should do things better and how you're not doing them right, now. Listen to the voice and you'll find that it has no positive elements in its opinion of you. It needs for you to do it their way, because according to the voice, you obviously aren't doing it right.

Usually, by the time we notice it, the voice has been growing and cultivating inside of us for many years now which has caused it to become a very strong part of your life. The good news is that we're going to learn not only how to diminish this voice, but keep it from holding you back any longer.

When you go after anything worthwhile in your life, the voice is going to rear its ugly head and tell you that you'd better stop now or you're only looking for disappointment at the end. It wants you to fail. Why? Because ultimately you'll have to rely more on the voice for direction; which is exactly what it wants. The voice needs you to fail so it can remain in control. That's its only objective. Has the voice ever been anything but negative? So the limited choices it gives you are to make sure that you end up in failure and defeat. Why? So it can keep you under its thumb, so it can be right. That's its only motivation.

This inner voice is the reason why so many well-intentioned people who really want to improve and better their lives end up failing. This inner voice is that strong and that impactful. So if you find yourself a week to three months into a project or goal which you really want to accomplish something you know will make you feel amazing and alive, ready to tackle the world head on, this inner voice is going to start softly and periodically speaking to you from within, giving you nothing but negative reinforcement.

At first, the voice will be tiny and soft. Very soon it will become larger, looking for ways to get you to start skipping a day, putting off until tomorrow what you need to accomplish now. This voice will start off acting like it's your friend and has only your best interests at heart. And soon it will get louder, and often times it will sound more reasonable in its rationale as to why you should forget your goals and stop everything now.

And if you listen to the voice, eventually you will stop. You'll begin to find ways to accept it and acknowledge that it's right. You will give it merit. However, you can put an end to the voice. Later in the chapter on *Managing That Nagging Voice For Good*, we're going to make that voice work for you, and not against you.

— FINISH LINE EXERCISE —

Tools to Calm the Nagging Inner Voice

Your goal here is to really create as much of a complete person as possible. Together, we are going to give this voice an identity.

▶ What does your voice look like?

▶ Give it a face.

▶ Give the voice a personality as big as you can.

Is there a time period you can attach to the voice? For example, when you put a hair style and clothing to the voice.

Is this person someone who dresses like they were from the sixties, seventies, eighties?

Choose a decade.

TIP: Make sure you address all the above traits. Try to make as detailed a persona as you can.

In the next exercise we are going to learn to manage your inner voice. NOTE: Not everyone has the same issues with their inner voice so this exercise may have different results for you.

Do You Feel Less Significant Than Others?

"We judge ourselves by what we feel capable of doing, while others judge us by what we have already done."

- Henry Wadsworth Longfellow

People can often be self-conscious when they're in public. They'll actually look at themselves through another person's eyes. You may wonder if your hair looks alright, or how you look in that dress. Yet at the same time we all crave contact. We want to be with other people. It's in our nature to interact with others, so we endure how we think we're being perceived and go out into the world anyway.

The funny thing about this is that most people are so worried about themselves that they often don't have time to judge others. Test this out. Have you ever walked down the isle of a store and found someone standing right in the middle, causing you to either stop and wait for them to move or to navigate around them? They didn't even acknowledge or realize you were there. Or, maybe they saw you at the very last moment and mouthed the words "I'm sorry" and then moved away. I'm sure this has happened to you before. Maybe you became resentful that you were ignored like that. After all, you're a human being too. Have you experienced something like this? Usually, they're actually a nice person. But they were so preoccupied with their own thoughts that they didn't notice the world around them.

There may be times when you're walking down the street and someone else is walking towards you and looks at you. You wonder if they're noticing your hair, shoes, clothing, or the way you walk.

Is something out of place? Do I have food in my teeth? It may never occur to you that they might be wondering what you think of them!

Everyone has two thoughts in times like this; how do others perceive me, and how do I perceive others? One is a need to fit in. The other is a judgment based upon how we view others, based on our view of how the world should be. Neither is right or wrong. But both can hold you back. When we choose to constantly worry about how others view us it can keep the creative juices from flowing. This type of thinking can keep you from thinking outside the box. It can also stress you out and keep your vision limited.

If you can keep in mind that these are just "perceived" judgments, then you can focus on what's in front of you.

What If This Program Doesn't Work For Me?

"When you get into a tight place and everything goes against you, till it seems you cannot hold on a minute longer, never give up then for that is just the place and time the tide will turn."

- Harriet Beecher Stowe

After testing and retesting my program with people who have tried my five simple *Power Principles*, the methods have proven to be sound. The success rate of people who use all five of the *Power Principles* to achieve more in their lives is outstanding. But it's important to practice all five of the *Power Principles*.

Think of it as if you were flying a plane. If you start the engine but don't put the throttle down, it won't move. If you put the throttle down but don't release the brakes, you'll never take off. And if you don't steer the plane and pull back on the yoke you won't get very far.

By now you may be saying: "I've done the principles of other people's programs and they haven't worked. Why will yours work?" One reason why so many other programs fail to work is that there's sometimes too much for you to do and often too much information to absorb when you're already faced with life's daily chores, tasks, and obligations. Even though all of the new exercises they ask you to do are good and have real merit, they're hard to keep up with in a consistent routine so that you stay motivated and on track. Another reason why people fail in other programs is that doing them independently can often lead to people losing their passion.

That's why I've developed principles that are very basic and simple to incorporate into your life that address the reasons behind these failures. And that's why the power of a *group* is a key element for driving you forward. Now I will stress that in life there is no magic bullet and that you cannot merely sit with this book on your chest and get the benefits it offers through osmosis. You'll have to put some time and effort into this. But the main difference is that the *Power Principles* are simple to do, and don't require a great deal of time to achieve results. Over time, you may find that they work so well for you on such a basic level that you're actually devoting more time to them because you're seeing great results, greater benefits, and the rewards they have to offer you.

— *Framework* —

The tools of the *5 Power Principles* using the Foundation of CORE

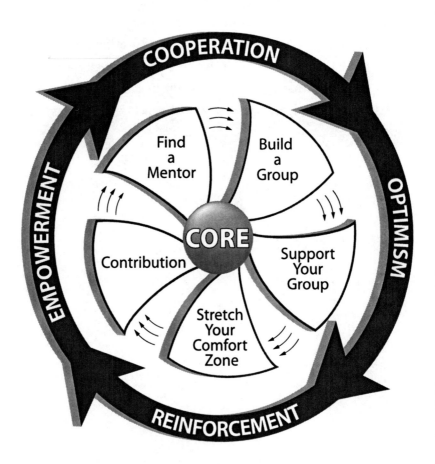

Part 2 —
Building A New
Foundation

CORE - Understanding How To Use It

C - Cooperation: You are part of a unit that must all work together towards a common goal: Success.

O - Optimism: You support them, they support you. In this way you work together to strengthen one another and build confidence.

R - Reinforcement: Let the people in your unit know how they're progressing. This builds strong foundations of accomplishment. Don't offer false compliments.

E - Empowerment: Encourage others in your group by keeping them on the right track towards their goals.

So what exactly is CORE and why is it important for you?

CORE is the foundation of this program. It's the driving force that gives you the power you need to accomplish anything. Power Principle One says: Build a Group. In essence, this is what your CORE will be for you. These are people who will give you the strength to keep moving forward. They are comprised of people with goals similar to your own. But there are several criteria when choosing these people. When finding people for your CORE they need to be people who inspire and instill confidence and who do not use their CORE to dump their own emotions and problems onto. And neither should you. While there may be times when you find that you are commiserating on a particular issue that may be blocking your progress, the objective with your CORE is to get constructive feedback that helps you push through a blocked or tough area which causes you to slow your progress. And you need to look for ways to encourage the others in your CORE to work through and push past their limiting beliefs as well. You will act almost as a mini-mentor for them because you will have an outside perspective and can often times see where their roadblocks are much more clearly than they can, because you're not as close to the inside of their circle as they are with their own issues. You don't have as much at stake, and therefore can see more clearly what they themselves might be missing.

Another aspect of working with your CORE will be learning to listen more effectively. Really make an effort to hear what the other person is saying, and not just get caught up in finding the solution. Sometimes by just listening, the solution will become apparent to the both of you.

Although listening and being present for the other person can be difficult to master, a good technique to help you do this is to take the word "I" out of your dialogue. Every time you begin to use the word "I", stop and reframe how you say something. When hearing another person in your CORE speak about a roadblock they're experiencing, it's easy and instinctive to talk about how you too have struggled with this same problem. Instead, take the "I" out of it and reframe your response. You can ask instead: "How does that make you feel?" "What do you think you can do about that?" "How are you going to handle it?" "Have you encountered someone with the same issues?" As you assist and help them to move forward, use phrases that engage the other person allowing them to examine their situation on a deeper level. When it's your turn you can then switch back to the "I" state.

> **SECRET:** Often when you keep the focus on the other person and really commit to helping and being present for them, you'll end up finding clarity for your own situation while addressing theirs.

By addressing your response in this way, you'll give the other person a chance to dig a little deeper and come to their own conclusions. That gives them a better sense of *self,* and allows them to see that the answers are often found inside. It also shows them that you're really engaged in listening to them and not just waiting to chime in and talk about your own experience. You are fully devoted to helping them figure out what is keeping them from moving forward and succeeding.

A good skill to acquire is empathy. In this regard, women are excellent nurturers. They come from a more compassionate spirit, where men are more likely to come from more pragmatic "Let's fix this" attitude. Practice speaking to each other in a more empathic way, focusing on the other person's needs can put both men and women on the right path.

When you do this, you unconsciously also give the other people in your CORE the tools they too can use to deal with obstacles in their own lives. Just by your listening, they're receiving powerful information for handling their own lives and moving forward.

Exercises For Expanding Your CORE

"You see, in life, lots of people know what to do, but few people actually do what they know . Knowing is not enough! You must take action."

- Tony Robbins

So how do you expand your CORE? You look for people who can support you in your goals. What does that mean? They're people who get what you are setting out to accomplish and either have similar goals and aspirations or have been through similar experiences. Sometimes it can be a mentor, but more often your CORE is filled with peers who also desire to climb to the next level and are on a path similar to your own.

And stretching your comfort zone (which also happens to be *Power Principle Three*), is an excellent way to develop your CORE. By getting out into the world and engaging with other people you may surprise yourself and find that you're meeting people at your level or slightly above. You never know where your next contact is going to come from. So, how do you do this? How do you meet new people who can impact your life and make a positive change? You need to get out of your comfort zone.

For Example: when you're in line at a store, take a look at the person in front or behind you and look at what they're purchasing. Is it something that you like as well? Is it a favorite food you have in common, or perhaps they have something that you've been curious about? What a great way to open a conversation! Does it look like they are planning for a party or event? Is there something in their basket that you've never seen before? These are all excellent ways to start asking questions and engaging. When someone has a couple bottles of wine, some cheese and fruits, etc. it may look like they're putting a party together. You could say something like; "Wow, I want to go to your party. Looks like it would be fun." Even if they aren't throwing a party it still breaks the ice and you are now engaged in conversation. Ask them if they live nearby. Did they just leave work to do their shopping? If you ask them about an unusual item in the cart, get curious and find out if they've used it before. Do they like it? What's the best way they know to use it?

Again, you're trying to find people who you could potentially add to your CORE so you want to look for commonalities or similar interests. Every encounter should be practice for you so it's not overwhelming when you first begin approaching new people. Remember, its progress not perfection. When you treat every encounter as if it was only practice, it will take the pressure off both you and the ultimate outcome of the situation.

If you're in line at the bank, look for something unique to compliment them on. It may be a unique watch, or their dress, suit, or shoes. Stretch your comfort zone and really put yourself out there. You might be surprised to find that the other person begins asking questions about you as well. This creates another opportunity for you to communicate. Anything new can feel awkward or uncomfortable in the beginning, but practice always makes us better. We find it gets easier as we do it.

Another way to accomplish this is to take a class, course, or seminar that you're interested in. This is a place your most likely to meet like-minded people. While it's not a requirement to find people who want the same things as you, you do, however, want to look for people who are on a similar path of wanting growth and advancement for themselves.

Remember, simple is often best. A genuine hello to someone can open some amazing doors of opportunity. So get out of your comfort zone and start taking chances!

Synergy Takes Practice

"Synergy - the bonus that is achieved when things work together harmoniously."

  - Mark Twain

Y ou are not going to get it right the very first time. In fact, finding a good CORE that supports you can take time. Remember when you first met some of the people who are your friends today? Or think back to when you were a kid. In the beginning you started as acquaintances until something or some event bonded you together. It may have been an incident or something in common you both shared, but it solidified your relationship and made you close friends. Sometimes it's something as simple as proximity. You happened to live close by each other. While you may find that the people in your CORE group have similar interests, you may also find that they don't all lend the type of support necessary for everyone's development. They may have similar goals but you notice that they're never available. Life consumes them too much and they cannot create a balance within their own lives. Therefore they are unable to find the time necessary for them to be present as part of your CORE on a consistent basis.

Now you may find that some people in your CORE don't have a great deal of time to lend to the group but, when they do have time it is valuable. You might have to grow the number of people in your CORE even more to keep them close but, not rely on some of them as much. It's okay to have anywhere from four to twenty or more people in your CORE. If you don't continue to expand your CORE you'll find that some of the people in your group who may not be as available as you'd like or need will let you down in ways that can only lead to setbacks. You do not want to spend your time worrying about why someone isn't as available. What you need to do is to have a big enough CORE so when someone cannot be present for you, you have enough additional people in your group to balance the empty times when you need their counsel most.

Note: you may be confused what your CORE is versus a team of people who can help you with your objectives. Your CORE are people who you get feedback from towards reaching your goal. A team are people who have the tools or resources to help you reach your goal (i.e. a web designer, copywriter, etc.). Team members can at times also be a mentor or someone within your network.

What Makes The Top One Percent Successful?

"There is no point at which you can say 'Well I'm successful now. I might as well take a nap.'"

- Carrie Fisher

I examined the reasons behind why so many people are not able to reach their dreams, their goals, or their desires. I couldn't understand how with so much self-help and self-improvement material out there in the form of books, courses, tapes, CDs, DVDs, and seminars, why so many people were unable to achieve their dreams. And it wasn't just a few people. Why? The question bugged and nagged at me. Was this on purpose? Did the world of self-help want people to fail? If so, for what reason? Did they want people to stay addicted to self-improvement materials and never go beyond their current status? I didn't think so. It didn't make sense. I'd read so many of these books myself and the message was always good and the tools were always useful. I was perplexed.

So when I began teaching people how to reach their goals and become successful, I was looking at the failure rate and what was keeping people from climbing the ladder. Was it something they were born with? Was it in their genes? Couldn't be. There were too many people who struggled with bad genes for that to be their cause of failure, and of course there was no scientific data to enforce and support that theory. And this theory was disproved every time someone I knew overcame their hurdles and reached the finish line. But still there were too few people succeeding. It frustrated me to no end to understand why. People from all walks of life have the ability to learn, to achieve, to better themselves. It's been proven time and time again. So what was holding the rest back? Why are there such a small percentage of people who were successful?

When examining the factors behind that question I looked at their lifestyles, the accessibility of education and the money that was available to them. I even looked at opportunity and luck. Even though, I personally don't believe in luck. I think opportunity comes because we have drive and the skills needed to succeed. Skills can always be learned. Of course I may never be an astronaut, but have you ever heard of someone becoming an astronaut because of luck? Opportunity maybe, training and skill, but not luck.

Then, while studying the traits of achievers in the top one percent, I began to notice a pattern. Even Malcolm Gladwell touches upon it in his book Outliers: "Successful people don't do it alone. Where they come from matters. They're products of particular places and environments. Bill Gates and the Beatles owe their genius to nurture not nature."

These people all seemed to have a solid family or relationship background. They came from a strong family foundation of parents and siblings who inspired and encouraged them. These families made them feel whole, complete, and gave them the support to build confidence within themselves so that when they went into the world they felt like they could handle anything. It wasn't that they were cocky or conceited; it was more that they were in-tune with the world and this resonated with people and life. Being part of a strong, healthy family gave them the same attitude when encountering anyone they met. They treated everyone with respect, importance, and value. And they were not afraid to approach people and engage with them.

I also noticed some of the top people didn't necessarily come from a big or strong family upbringing, but had a great marital relationship with the support and encouragement from their spouse and children. The family that the two of them created helped to give them a solid foundation. In turn, their new families helped create within them the power and support to handle the world around them and participate in it.

And, still others had amazing friendship bonds that grew in college. These bonds they created survive to this day as their close friends, business partners, confidants, and mentors continue to encourage and support them. The ties are strong, bound by the time they spend together, almost like a unit of the military. If you were in a fraternity or sorority the bond was even greater. You had a sense of pride, honor, accomplishment, and support. Entrepreneurs like Bill Gates and Paul Allen of Microsoft, and Steve Jobs and Steve Wozniak of Apple fame, are famous examples of such people and these relationships.

Though the people I mention above also continued their relationships into and through the business world, there are others who've established their strong relationships in business with partners and associates. This can often happen with first year lawyers who spend hours in the trenches at a new firm, or first year doctors and interns, who experience life-challenging demands required of them. By the time they go through this experience, the bonds they've created with their associates become exceptionally strong - a force to be reckoned with.

There are also those courageous people who serve in the military, who also posses these very same qualities of a strong bond. They serve in a unit together, where they are broken down and depleted of every self-serving belief they possessed which could make them rebellious and ineffective to their unit. They spend many hours together training, exercising, and taking care of their weapons. They eat together, sleep together, shower together, and fight together as a unit. They watch each other's backs and everyone is expected to do the same. If someone slips up or steps out of line, everyone pays the consequences. Why? To illustrate how one person is no more or no less important than the others in their unit, and how one's actions has consequences for all. They are a single unit, and no one will let them forget that. No one is left behind.

It's also a major reason why so many soldiers who return home to civilian life from their tour of duty to their wives, children, and loved ones, have trouble fitting back into society. It's not because they don't love and care about their families, in fact these are the very people they were fighting to protect and keep safe. And, their difficulties reacclimating are not always because they experience so much trauma from war, although that can be a big factor for some. They have trouble feeling like they belong because they've been separated from their unit who they lived with 24-hours a day. Separated from the very people they fought side-by-side with for months or even years, and sometimes also as a result of multiple tours of duty.

Of course, there are soldiers who do go back to civilian life and are just fine, but you'll notice that these people are primarily the ones who came from strong familial ties. Their ability to continue on with life as they were is because they came from good, solid family foundations. Of course, there are cases when the trauma of war becomes too much for anyone to endure.

The people who are most successful in life are oftentimes the ones who are buoyed to their background of strong familial relationships. They are formidable foes of loss and defeat and are always up for any challenge. Think of the creators and innovators of our country, and you'll find people who have a solid sense of self and probably an even stronger family or relationship background.

As you reach deeper into this book, you'll find the tools that will give you the foundation to learn how to acquire these skills. Even though you may not have had these skills growing up, you can learn them in an easy and manageable way, that will become a strong foundation for you.

When you combine this process with the other 5 *Power Principles* which are all easy to learn, you will find yourself going after everything you set your sights on, and master it. Possibly for the first time in your life, you'll find that you are completing a higher percentage of the things you focus on. Your success rate will increase and you will be on your way to the top!

Developing A New Muscle

"Be not afraid of growing slowly, be afraid only of standing still."
   - Chinese Proverb

Right now, you are building a new muscle. Building your CORE and practicing the 5 *Power Principles* is going to stretch your comfort zone and will develop new muscles for you to have and use. At first, practicing the *Power Principles* may seem awkward and unfamiliar to you, even counterintuitive. As you get better at stretching your comfort zone and challenging yourself by meeting new people and taking greater risks, you are going to be forming a practice that will eventually become part of your daily routine. Soon it will become second nature as easy as buttoning your shirt.

Is something preventing you from following through right now? Procrastination is such a fickle beast. Why is jumping in and doing something new so daunting to us? Why, for some, does every challenge seem like we're climbing the Himalayas? It could be writing a resume, filing out an application, organizing the pantry, changing the oil in your car, doing your homework, cooking, cleaning, shopping, washing the clothes, filing paperwork, writing that thesis, paying the bills, writing that book, or throwing a party.

Whether it's work or pleasure, tasks can often look overwhelming and foreboding to us and we dread just sneaking up on them and beginning. So we procrastinate, and watch a TV show before tackling that project. Then it turns into two shows, then three, and before you know it, it's time for bed. You may say to yourself; "Today work was a bit tougher than usual. So I'll start my projects tomorrow." Sometimes our avoidance at beginning a project is so strong that we'd even do some other menial task as an excuse not to begin right away. But what's really going on here?

Now, do we have the same avoidance response when we have help from others or when doing a project along with someone else? Not often, and not as much. So it's not always the task at hand that's the problem. The problem for some can be in doing a task or project alone. Have you ever had pack-up for a move or paint a house or apartment you recently moved into? Not fun by yourself. You come up with many excuses to avoid doing the work. How do you (creatively) get around that roadblock? You entice your friends with pizza to come over and pitch in. Because when we have the support of others the task becomes less daunting. By making a task into a party, it becomes more fun.

So how do you learn to tackle a project or goal on your own? Although it's true that writing a thesis or outlining a presentation for work can be a big project that you might be dreading, there's a difference between finding an excuse not to do it – however poor it may be, and knowing that it's an overwhelming project and that you need to push forward and do it anyway.

SECRET: In college, why do some people study in the library? Clue: It's not just because there are books available. It's because being around other people's energy triggers your own energy. That's why your local coffee shop is filled with so many working and socializing people. The next time you are at your college library or local coffee house, notice how many are working or studying. It's not the coffee. I know many people who can't stand Starbucks coffee yet are there almost every day.

In his book "Eat That Frog", Brian Tracy refers to any task that seems big or overwhelming as the frog, the hardest thing on your plate that you have to eat. He suggests jumping in and eating that frog first. Why? The simplest answer is that tackling the hardest project first makes the others seem more manageable and easier to swallow. Earlier, I used the example of tackling your biggest bill first in order to see a clear path to significantly cutting the other projects down to a manageable size. To build a new muscle, you don't have to go after the entire project all in one sitting. But if you start, the momentum of that effort will soon pick up speed. Second, it's important for you to find ways to get you out of your isolation and elicit the help of others. These two techniques alone will create a shift in your "stall" process and make it easier to move forward on your projects and objectives.

Modeling Successful Behavior - What Winning Looks Like

"People rarely succeed unless they have fun in what they are doing."

\- Dale Carnegie

Think back to when you first began to learn something new, when you were a young child. Let's say you were someone who wanted to play just like the professional football players do. So how did you begin acquiring these skills? Well, you may have had a parent who showed you what to do. For me, my mother was a tomboy and taught me baseball, basketball, and football. That person would show you how to hold the ball at the laces, how to cock your arm back just so, and how to release the ball from your fingertips so you could achieve a good spin on the ball. Or perhaps you saw a sports game on TV, ran out to the yard and immediately tried to model and imitate the behavior of the players you saw on the screen.

At such a young age, we are mimickers. You didn't know quite what you were doing, and yet you kept imitating these mannerisms until it became natural to you. And even though you may have lacked the fundamentals of fully understanding the concepts to help hone your skills, you weren't too bad. But you knew that if you really wanted to get good at this, you'd need a much deeper understanding of how to execute whatever you took on. So you started to seek out people who had the answers and knew more about it than you did. You start asking questions.

Sometimes these very same people would not always know how to really do it right either, but they still offered advice because everyone likes giving advice to someone. But we all have instincts and you could often tell when you weren't quite getting all the tutoring you really needed to excel to the next level. So you began to focus on seeking out an expert. Someone who really knew how it worked. You started looking for a mentor.

So what exactly is a mentor? A mentor is someone who has the skill and experience in a particular field you also have an interest in. They likely (and preferably) have achieved a certain level of success at what they do in that field.

What type of person achieves success on a continuous basis?

When you think of winning, do you think of someone like Michael Phelps, the Olympic swimmer who won fourteen gold medals? Or is it completing an assignment at work? Finishing that painting? Completing that exercise program? Successfully providing for your family? What does winning mean for you?

Is winning only meaningful to you if other people acknowledge your accomplishment? Or, is it enough for you to be satisfied with the results? This is an important distinction for what *really* motivates you. One is a constant inner force that drives you and moves you forward. The other only motivates you when someone else is aware of your current progress. Neither motivation is necessarily good or bad, but it helps to be aware of what the *motivation* <u>indicators</u> are that push and drive you forward.

How Can You Tell When It's Working?

"A man can succeed at almost anything for which he has unlimited enthusiasm."

- Charles M. Schwab

There are several signs you may notice that indicate you're making progress. One is that you have more energy. Another is that you're enjoying your alone time. You are taking in life and enjoying the process. When you're driving home and are stuck on the freeway, you actually find yourself enjoying the sunset, or admiring the trees. You're more relaxed. More contemplative. You may get up earlier in the day and stay at work later, and find yourself enjoying it. You're making every action count. Another sign you're progressing is that you want to be around people and participate in society more. You are constantly striving to move forward and upwards. You are up for bigger and better challenges. And you are looking forward to newer challenges.

One of the most important elements for achieving any kind of success is knowing what you want for yourself. You're going to need to know specifically what your goals are, what you're willing to accept in your life and what the life you desire looks like to you. To do this effectively, you're going to need to get very specific. There's an old saying: "Don't talk about the fruit, describe the apple." In other words, if you're vague and abstract about the results you want, then your goals are going to be cloudy at best. The more detailed you can be about your objectives, the more visual and real your goal will become, and the greater the results your results will be.

Aren't you more specific when you're preparing to buy or lease a new car? You don't just say I want a car - you already have a model and color in mind. You've probably also pictured yourself in the driver's seat, imagining what it would be like to actually own and drive this car. Imagining yourself already participating in an experience is the greatest way of manifesting what you want in your life. You can even take this step farther. When I know what car I want, I picture myself at the gas station filling up the tank. Again, the more clear the vision of your goal is, the more specific you're imagining, the more likely you are going to be moving toward your objective.

Have you noticed how sales people always attempt to get you to picture yourself already owning their products? Car salesmen have you sit in and actually drive the vehicle. Some Real Estate agents will have a pie or cookies baking in the kitchen to get your senses working. They may light or warm the rooms of a house to evoke feelings of comfort and familiarity within you, to give you the sensation that you're already home. The same technique also works for adopting a new puppy or dog, selling you new golf clubs, or purchasing a new suit. The salesperson will let you play and bond with the dog. The savvy golf salesperson will let you handle the clubs and take practice swings like you're already on the course. The master salesperson will have you try on and get comfortable with that new suit, seeing how great you look in the mirror. They all know that once you put yourself into the experience and actually feel the sensations associated with having and possessing these things, it becomes even harder to resist.

If you want to become great at manifesting, this is a practice that you'll want to hone for everything else in your life. Whether your goal is to be more fit and in great shape, or to have an amazing relationship with your soul mate, or to have an incredible career, or to have unlimited wealth and success, getting specific about what you want can have incredible results. The more specific and detailed you can be about your goal, the more likely you are to see your goal as achievable.

Your brain is an *Experience Simulator* -

Without having to do something you could simulate it...

Here are some examples:

➢ Diving off a cliff

➢ Winning the lottery

➢ Going on vacation

➢ Asking a top model out

➢ Buying a fast food dinner

We've all heard of *Flight Simulators*. This is a process that takes you through what it would be like if you were actually sitting at the controls of a plane. On a very simplistic level, this can be done through your computer using a software program. On a more sophisticated level, training pilots will strap into large machines which replicate an actual plane in flight. From there we can begin to understand about Ride Simulators.

Ride Simulators, typically found at amusement parks, rely on proprioceptors which are receptors located in your muscles, tendons, joints and the inner ear, which send signals to the brain regarding the body's position. An example of a "popular" proprioceptor often mentioned by aircraft pilots is the "seat of the pants". Proprioceptors respond to stimuli generated by muscle movement and muscle tension. Signals generated by exteroceptors and proprioceptors are carried by sensory neurons or nerves and are called electrochemical signals.

When a neuron receives such a signal, it sends it on to an adjacent neuron through a bridge called a synapse. A synapse "sparks" the impulse between neurons through electrical and chemical means. These sensory signals are processed by the brain and spinal cord, which then respond with motor signals that travel along motor nerves. Motor neurons, with their special fibers, carry these signals to muscles, which are instructed to either contract or relax. In other words, these sensors present a picture to your brain as to where you are in space as external forces act on your body.

For example, picture yourself sitting at a red traffic light in your car. The light changes to green and your foot presses the accelerator. As you accelerate away from the traffic light, you will "feel" yourself being pushed back in to the seat. That experience is transmitted to your brain via the proprioceptors, in particular, through the sensors in your backside and back. The brain interprets this information as an acceleration in the forward sense. If you now slam on the brakes to stop suddenly, you will find different proprioceptors at work. The deceleration will be felt through your hands and feet and your backside will now be trying to slide forward in the seat. This information is again presented to your brain and thus it interprets the deceleration taking place. In turn, the brain now signals the muscles in your arms and legs to contract and stop you from sliding forward in the seat.

I apologize for getting so technical, but a similar sensation takes place in your brain through *Experience Simulators*. Before you even get out of your house, get up from your chair, or put your clothes on, you think about an experience such as going to a dinner party, or to the movies. Or perhaps driving home in traffic, or rushing out to pick up dinner or your dry cleaning in rush hour traffic. Sometimes through *Experience Simulators* you might begin to anticipate or maybe even dread going out and doing these things because you've already simulated the experience in your mind and through previous experiences have decided either that it will be fun or what's the point?

We use *Experience Simulators* on a daily basis. In fact, we do this all day long. When you're hungry you imagine what to have for lunch. Since you may have time constraints you even picture the shortest route to your destination. You picture yourself at the drive thru or sitting down to have a meal. Biting into that burger or sandwich. Then you think and imagine possibly having a salad instead. We do this all the time through *Experience Simulators*.

Through *Experience Simulation* we can use this powerful mind tool to help us to reach our goals. You can also begin to see what success will feel like and through simulating these experiences in your mind. You can also begin to prepare yourself for the journey and all the steps necessary to get you to your goal by visualizing what direction you need to take and the proper tools you'll need to help you get there.

Gauge Your Progress Through Visualization

"I saw it and had to have it. I didn't know exactly what the road to my dream would look like, or how tough the journey would be, but I knew I had to have it."

- Craig S. Copeland

One of the key elements for success in any improvement course is gauging your progress. How do you do this? Setting goals on paper is an excellent way to see how far you're progressing. When you build your CORE, you'll use what you've written down to get an idea of how far you've progressed. Keeping it in your head is not going to work. Your head will get overloaded at times with daily things like work, chores, projects, and errands, and you'll be hard-pressed to keep your list of goals at the top of your thoughts. Also, by writing them down on a piece of paper and displaying it in a prominent place, you reinforce your goals in your mind and get a better picture of how best to accomplish them.

With all five of our senses constantly in use, you can see in a heartbeat how easily distracted we get by even the slightest of noises, smells, sights, tastes, or touch. And because we're so easily distracted, it's vital to have your goals and objectives written down where you can see them. In this way, you no longer have problems when everything gets off course. When life throws you a curve; then; flat tire,... heavy traffic,... overslept,... pretty woman, or handsome man passing by, you won't get derailed from your goal because it's now right there in front of you, making it your most important objective and greatest success.

Also, by looking at your goals on a regular basis, you take more ownership of them and it's more likely that you will be conscious of where you presently are in relation to them. You're also much more likely to manifest something into reality when you look at it daily rather than keeping it locked in your mind.

Setting Reachable Goals

"Do not let what you cannot do interfere with what you can do."

\- John Wooden

An important part of progress is to envision a minimal failure rate. We all have something we do well now, even if it's programming a TiVo to record shows for you (which for a lot of people is a major accomplishment). All of us have something that we do so well and get satisfaction from. If you think about it, you've probably also received a compliment about that thing you do well at some point in your life. Someone may have told you: You're such a good writer. No one bakes like you do. The way you designed your house is amazing. That was a wonderful party you threw. You're a really good friend. You're always so thoughtful of others. Tapping into those memories helps you to identify and acknowledge that you are already doing something well. Acknowledging this is a key component to heightening your abilities to try something new. As you put yourself into this state, you will instantly tap into your core confidence and make it that much easier to tackle something new.

What are reachable goals? Starting a new business? Buying a new house? Getting a degree? Finding your soul mate? Redecorating your home? Becoming a better writer, speaker, or artist? This is going to be different for everyone. As you work towards your goals, you are going to need to see progress to maintain your drive, energy, and momentum. The best way to do this is to get feedback from your CORE, but it's important that you don't use them as your only source of feedback. You can get a sense of praise and progress from inside of yourself as well. What your CORE can do better than anyone is to give you valuable information on how to tweak your progress even more, with insights into better techniques in order to develop even greater successes. Your CORE can provide you with valuable information on how you're progressing, through eyes different than your own. Outside objectivity can give you greater clarity, which in turn will improve your direction with laser focus.

Procrastinate No More

"If you advance confidently in the direction of your dreams and endeavor to live the life which you have imagined, you will meet success unexpected in common hours."

- Henry David Thoreau

Are you someone who procrastinates? If so, why exactly don't you like to see something to completion? What is it about the project that seems worse to you than eating live bugs? Even if you do procrastinate, can you remember completing something big that you took on in the past? What did that feel like to you? Didn't it feel like a great accomplishment and made you feel pretty good about yourself? So we have established that it can be rewarding and fulfilling when you reach the finish line.

Don't forget to set time limits for each assignment, write them down on a piece of paper and display in a place where you'll see and refer to it until you complete each task. As you accomplish these tasks, you'll put the date and time of completion next to each one. You'll also put a checkmark in front of the task or cross it out, but leaving it legible so you can see what the specific task was. There is something quite satisfying about seeing the results of a completed objective.

When you have accomplished each of these tasks, start a new sheet and write eight to ten items to be accomplished on this one. These should be goals or tasks you want or need to see completed.

You'll notice that the tasks above are things that almost everyone needs to do anyway. The objective here is to choose small tasks in the beginning so you can build up the discipline and see progress of accomplishment in your life. Your desired outcome is to create habits of completion in a timely fashion.

What if you're already someone who does things well and are not a procrastinator? If you've picked up this book to help you finish what you start, I can only surmise that while smaller tasks are easy for you to handle, your big goals seem further away and harder to achieve. A house gets built one nail at a time. A race is won one step at a time. And a frog is eaten one bite at a time. Perhaps it's time for you to set your table, put a plate down, chose the proper fork and knife, perhaps add some salt, and a napkin. All metaphorically speaking, of course.

As with any new habit, repetition and seeing it through to the end helps to build a foundation of completion. As you become more proficient, you'll naturally begin to tackle bigger and greater challenges. So, start small but continue to take on bigger tasks. Completing them will give you the mental attitude of success and you'll find yourself stepping into the next task with the drive and determination to see it through to the end.

Managing That Nagging Inner Voice For Good

"The gem cannot be polished without friction, nor man perfected without trials."

- Confucius

Taming and then eliminating that nagging inner voice will do wonders to take your foot off the brake allowing you to increase your drive and energy toward creating unstoppable success. Some parts of the process toward getting rid of your nagging inner voice may seem contradictory to you or perhaps even silly, but they're necessary if you want to finally get rid of a major roadblock.

The first step is to begin by recognizing your nagging inner voice, and identify it when it rears its ugly head. The moment you start to hear that voice, stop to recognize it. Get out that little pad and pencil that you can carry with you, and make note of that voice whenever it appears. Write down the date and time it shows up and what specifically it wants you NOT to do. Remember, that voice is not on your side, so there is always something it doesn't want you to do or accomplish. Please keep in mind that it's only there to celebrate your failures, not your successes.

The second thing you'll do is begin to identify whose voice it is. Put a face to the voice and then give it sound. Whose voice is it? Start to examine how long you've had this voice within you. You may want to start a journal. You'll begin to see a pattern of when you started to have more failures and fewer successes in your life. You'll want to give the inner voice as much personality as you can because the more you can identify it and make it clear inside your head; the sooner you'll begin to eliminate it.

We can't get rid of what we can't see or understand, so you need to create as much of a personality for the inner voice as you possibly can. What does it look like? How does it sound? Is the voice male or female? What color is its hair? Does it wear pants or dresses? Is the voice loud or soft?

Now that you know how the voice looks, sounds, and acts, ask yourself if this voice is someone you know. It may very likely be a family member, or someone else from your past. Once you have established this, now you have a name to go with it. If you just can't come up with someone, then make up a name.

Now, when you begin to do something, anything that provokes the voice to appear, stop and immediately say to it: "Shhhh..." At first, the voice is not going to be quiet. It's been with you for many years and is used to being in charge. So it's going to take some time to control. But you can do this. The reason you are going to say "Shhhh" or "hush," is that you're going to build a routine to counteract the voice when it appears, diminish it, and eventually make it behave. This is called an *interrupt pattern*. It interrupts the way you normally do things so you can replace it with new behaviors that empower you to succeed.

When you acknowledge the voice you are going to have conversations with it. You're going to begin letting the voice know that what it's been doing is no longer acceptable. Although the voice is a part of you and you love it, you must keep its behavior in check. What did I just say? You *love* it? Isn't that contradictory? Nope. This is exactly what you want. If you push the voice away, try to avoid it, and never address what it has done to you over the years, then you can never really get rid of it for good. It will always nag at you. What you're going to do now is identify it, acknowledge it, be compassionate towards it, and then love it and set it free. To do all of this, you have to confront and address it.

So now you want to start a healthy dialogue which, over time, will replace the negative inner voice's dialogue with positive reinforcement. This will give you back the power and strength to accomplish anything. When the voice begins talking, you need to say out loud, "Shhh, stop. This conversation is *unacceptable* to me. I love you, but until you can say something positive that I can use, I'm ending this conversation now."

The first thing that's going to happen is you're going to feel extremely silly saying this out loud. In the beginning it will feel contrived and even a little ridiculous to be speaking to this imaginary voice. But this voice is anything but imaginary. It's the very thing that has been keeping you down for years.

The voice will come to you at the most unlikely times and you need to identify it immediately and stop it in its tracks. From this point forward it's *you* who's going to be in control and in the driver's seat of this inner dialogue. Again, it may feel a little silly at first, but you're going to address the *inner* voice with your *outer* voice and let it know that it's behavior towards you is unacceptable. You'll lovingly tell it; "Shhh…" and immediately say aloud that while you love the voice, if it can't say anything positive to you then the conversation will need to end for now.

This bears repeating. This is going to take practice on your part. In the beginning it will go against your very nature. But as you keep practicing this exercise, you'll discover in a very short time that you're the one in control and that you're mastering how the conversation goes and how it makes you feel.

At some point, you may get angry with the voice and also at yourself for letting it live within you for so long. This is a natural reaction, and you need only to acknowledge it and keep moving forward. It's OK to be angry, but it's not OK to let that anger rule you. The objective here is to get to a place of confidence and self-control.

Once you become good at this dialogue, you'll notice how another amazing thing starts to happen: You'll start to see and review the conversations you have with real people and immediately notice the negative ones instantly, and start to desire only the positive ones in your life. You'll soon see which conversations help to support, and encourage you, and which ones are critical of you and hold you back. Yes, it is constructive to get different kinds of feedback from people, but there's a difference between criticism and useful feedback. One is an unsolicited opinion, and the other is useful information that keeps you on the right track to success.

Every time you hear the voice, I want you to immediately use these three steps to give it a brand new look and personality. This will take a little practice, but if you do this every day for a week, it will no longer be something that has hold over you any longer.

— FINISH LINE EXERCISE —

Here we are going to master the anxieties you have about your nagging inner voice. Every time it rears its head and speaks to you, you may find yourself sink a little lower. Today, we're going to start to change your reaction to it with a few simple techniques.

Find a place where you will not be disturbed. Take 10 minutes in a quiet area where you can either stand or lay down.

You may close your eyes for this exercise.

1. Take the voice you presently have for your inner voice and give it a high squeaky voice. You can make it a very high-pitched voice like Mickey Mouse or another silly character voice. Can you hear it? It should sound pretty funny to you.

2. Since you've created a face for the voice, Now give it really huge, ridiculous ears. Make them kind of floppy, like an elephant's. Color them if you want. Can you see them?

3. Now, take that image you've given the inner voice and reduce it WAY down to the size of a tiny postage stamp. Make it really tiny and small. Then push it far away. See it two blocks down the road, where it looks extremely miniscule.

▶ Practice this technique every day for 30 days.

TIP: There is nothing embarrassing about this exercise. This is about taking charge of your path. The more you can diminish the inner voice the greater control and momentum you will create.

Where Do I Find People To Support Me?

"It is one of the most beautiful compensations of life, that no man can sincerely try to help another without helping himself."

- Ralph Waldo Emerson

This will take a bit of effort on your part, but it's not hard to do. Getting out into the world is where you'll find people. And the majority of people you're going to find for your support group will be found in places where you have common interests. I regularly go to a community coffee shop and keep running into the same people and eventually we talk (always sooner than later for me, because I end up talking to everyone). Also, when I had my dog North, I belonged to a dog park and found many people with similar interests to me there. If you have a special interest or hobby then you are likely to meet people where other people with your interests congregate; it could be at a learning course, at school, an art class, a yoga studio or the gym. And you'll instantly find like-minded people when you're doing volunteer work.

The best way not to meet people is to isolate yourself. And the more you stay isolated -the more you keep your headphones on or your earplugs in, the more you stay in your bubble always texting or locked behind a computer screen, the more you'll miss out on opportunities to meet others. I often carry a book with me wherever I go because I enjoy reading, but I often find that people will start a conversation with me because they too have read the book or they're interested in it. Having a book is a great opener for conversation.

The reverse holds true as well - if you see someone with a book that interests you, ask them about it. How far along are they? Are they enjoying it? What made them pick it up? Have they read other books by the same author? Again, asking questions and engaging with other people are great ways to find and build your group.

To reiterate, don't look for people you can whine, complain, or commiserate with. This is what 12-step programs are for, and while they usually help a person to ease their pain and get through some very trying times, they're not always the best vehicle to learn to maximize your life. 12-step programs have helped so many people deal with dire situations. If you're presently in a 12-step program you should use the tools provided to work on getting past your pain, hurt, and loneliness. Your goal should be to learn how to take back some of the control of your life and move beyond any addictions that you or a loved one share. When you are ready to start climbing to the top of the success ladder, you are going to need another set of tools.

— *Framework* —

The tools of the *5 Power Principles* using the Foundation of CORE

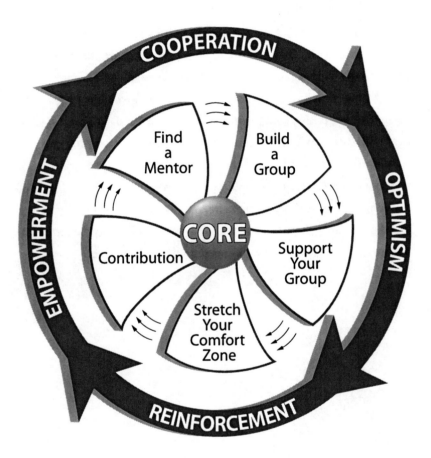

Part 3 — Creating Success That Sticks

The 5 Power Principles

"Opportunities multiple as they are seized."

   - Sun Tzu

The 5 *Power Principles* are the very essence of this success program. They are the key to your success in everything you do from now on. I have found that successful people use all five of these *Power Principles* together all the time, and that you cannot be successful using just one or two of them. I've broken them down into manageable, easy-to-follow steps that will take just a little time to learn and give you maximum results. The 5 *Power Principles* are:

- **BUILD A GROUP** - This group will be the foundation for helping you raise your esteem and motivate you to help keep you moving forward towards your objective.

- **SUPPORT YOUR GROUP** - Giving your group members encouragement to move forward benefits, empowers, and drives them, and supporting others benefits you as well.

- **STRETCH YOUR COMFORT ZONE** - Getting out of your comfort zone by pushing past your limits and creating a pattern of fear-breaking empowerment creates a stronger, more empowered you.

- **CONTRIBUTION** - Giving back to the world and your community helps to elevate yourself while helping others to grow and allows them the much needed opportunity to get back on their feet.

- **FIND A MENTOR** - Mentors who live life at a higher level help you maximize your personal growth and reach your goals.

Defining The 5 Power Principles

"Excellence is the result of caring more than others think is wise, risking more than others think is safe, dreaming more than others think is practical, and expecting more than others think is possible."

    - Unknown

By now you've had an overview of what these principles are. Throughout this book you've been given examples of some of each of these principles put into application and how they can benefit you. But there's more. Once you have all the ingredients for the *dynamite* that's going to drive your life to newer, even greater heights, what do you do with the actual dynamite itself? Yes! Light the fuse! It's within the process of lighting the fuse that you ignite your own power. It's the CORE to everything. So now let's examine each of these *Power Principles*, one by one.

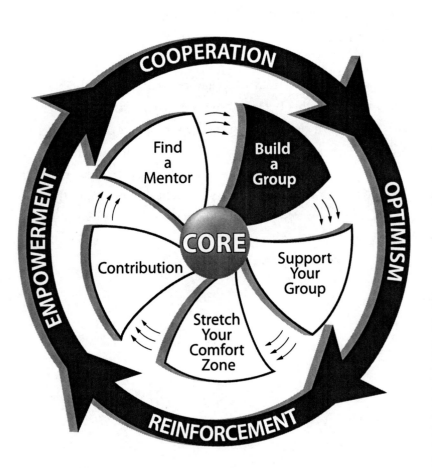

POWER PRINCIPLE

❶

BUILD A GROUP

These are the people who will act as your support, your family, your CORE.
Select people who will give you positive feedback and be present in your
life. Personal interaction is key. Create a network of support.

The Foundations Of Support

"Sometimes our light goes out but is blown into flame by another human being. Each of us owes deepest thanks to those who have rekindled this light."

   - Albert Schweitzer

As mentioned earlier, find people who you look forward to talking to. You probably have people like this in your life already. As I've said from the very beginning, you may already be doing a number of the principles on an unconscious level. If you are, the best thing you can do is to become more consciously aware of how you use them because after you've checked in with a member of people within your CORE, you want to gauge how each encounter went for you.

You want to look for several key things when you talk to someone who may be a good candidate for your CORE. First, you want to let the other person know about something that's happening in your life. It can be a project you're working on, a relationship in your life, something you experienced or did recently (an event, dinner, a show, etc.), or anything you would like to get the other person's feedback about. Typically, you'll bring up something that's related specifically to one of your goals or objectives.

One of the best ways to gauge our progress and accelerate our growth towards success is to check in with other people and get an objective view of how we're doing. This can occur when you call a friend on the phone. During that call, you let the other person know where you are in your life and listen to their feedback on how you're progressing. It's very important that you check in with someone who has typically been a supportive person in your life or can be a new support person for you. Do not choose a family member who may be critical of you and always seems to have a better way for you to do things. Steer clear of people with whom you're constantly trying to illicit that one positive response from, like a family member or someone else whose approval you are seeking, knowing that in your heart it may never come. When we speak with this type of personality, we typically end up feeling dejected and less than. This is not what you want to strive for.

Everyone has different relationships with their family and you'll have to decide if your people are supportive of you or mostly critical of you. Your objective is not to prove to them that you are a great person and to hear them say that, because you may never get that reaction from a critical family member. However well intentioned they think they are, some families support ends up coming across as criticism and disapproval. They may have never learned how to say something in a positive, constructive way. It's not necessarily their fault, but your objective is to find people who strengthen and empower you, and encourage you to keep pushing forward because you're on the right track.

Seek out people who are either at your level of success or slightly above and are also working on progressing, growing, and reaching new heights. Why? Because they will challenge and push you to do your best and keep working at reaching your goals. Secondly, they may be at a place where they too are experiencing or have already gone through what you're working on. They may have some constructive insights based upon their own recent experiences and how they got through to the next level. This information could be most valuable for you to hear.

When you're talking with a member of your CORE, give them an account of where you are now and what you are up to. Be sure to give the other person information about what obstacles you've come across, what you've accomplished, and what direction you want to take. Listen to yourself as you share your progress. How does your voice sound? How is your attitude? When speaking, is your mood improving or getting low? Strive to give the other person positive accounts of how you've done thus far. If you've encountered hurdles, how have you managed to get beyond them?

Down the road you may be able to have healthy, supportive conversations with your family. But for now, you'll want to find people who already speak in a language of support and love. I'm not suggesting that your family doesn't love or support you but more often than not, they can convey it in a less than supportive sounding, sometimes critical way. If they're worried about your job or finances, they may give you suggestions and advice about where to live, what you should do for work, and how you should live your life. Often this will make you feel underrated and misunderstood. While their intentions come from love, the words and convictions can sound harsh.

When you're working with someone in your CORE, don't use that time to dump your emotions or to complain or whine about something that's not good in your life. You can find some time to do this if it's really required at a later time, but for this specific meeting you want to come away from the session with some forward momentum behind you. At the end of the conversation you want the power of feeling motivated to keep you moving forward. Your objective is to create a positive outcome.

The support you are learning about here in this book is the kind of support that gives you the strength and power to live your life on your terms, and to start to live up to your full potential. My hope is to give you the tools necessary to maximize your life and accomplish anything you desire. Your goals are no longer unreachable, but now it's a matter of how you get started and when.

When you build your CORE you're building a group that encourages you to venture out on your own with the skills, attitude, and confidence to know that you're going to reach your goals. Your CORE should not act as a crutch, but more like a barometer to gauge where you are and how far you've progressed. They are here to give you constructive feedback and positive reinforcement.

Communicating With Others

"The single biggest problem in communication is the illusion that it has taken place."

- George Bernard Shaw

L et me ask you something. Does it bother you when speaking to a store clerk or someone at the checkout stand and they don't look at you directly when speaking with you? Like there's something better or more pressing on their mind? It actually causes you to lose connection with that person. Almost as if you're not important enough to them as a customer and that it didn't matter to them whether you made a purchase or not. When you engage in communication with someone and you don't look at them while they're speaking, when your attention is elsewhere, you convey this very same message that you are not interested in that person and what they have to say.

It breaks the connection and therefore any chance of building a deeper rapport with that person. Why would you want a deep rapport with someone? It's the connections within your life that are going to build your foundations, give you energy, put you in touch with resources that are pure gold for reaching your objectives, and create a fuller life for yourself. We as humans cannot exist independently forever. It's not in our nature to do so. What you always want to look for when creating success in your life and building a team of people and a network of connections that are going to help you accomplish your goals, is to build deep rapport with everyone whom you come into contact with. Who wouldn't want to help someone they have great rapport with?

There is an art to communication and it's not hard to do. It just takes practice, and getting into new habits. It's not about spending the entire time with another person talking about yourself. In fact, to most people it's so important to share about what's going on in their lives that they totally neglect the other person.

I'm going to share with you some great tools that can make you a good listener, faster. They take a little practice, but as you use them you'll find it's not hard to become a great communicator by becoming an even better listener.

> **SECRET:** Some of the most interesting, fascinating, and engaging people in the world, talk less about themselves and are more interested in the people around them. They are not just waiting until it's their turn to speak. TIP: Make everyone you encounter feel like they are the most important person to you.

What is it like when one person isn't listening to conversational clues being thrown right at them? Here is an example of a dialogue between two people meeting at a restaurant and sitting side by side at the counter:

You: Hello.

Them: Hi.

You: Have you been here before?

Them: Actually this is my first time here. Just moved here from Florida.

You: Oh. I come here every week. I love this food. The burgers are great.

Right now the "you" in this conversation is clueless. Why? Because "you" just went into a "share about myself" mode. The person sitting next to you just gave you plenty of free information to follow up on. It's almost as if they're testing to see if you have the intelligence or social skills to capitalize on what's being said.

So what would be an alternative "right" thing to say?

Well... they mentioned that this is their first time in the restaurant and they've just moved here from Florida.

You could have properly "watered the seeds" by asking

a) How do they like the restaurant, area, etc?

b) How did they find it or hear about it?

c) What brought them here from Florida?

d) How long have they been in this area?

e) Where in Florida are they from?

f) How long did they live there?

g) What's it like there?

h) Are they living here now or just visiting?

The two short sentences in the beginning of this conversation give you tons of information to follow up on. There are tons of conversational topics beneath the surface that they've indirectly indicated they'd like to talk about.

If the "you" in this conversation has ever been the you reading this book, then you're not alone. All of us have done this at one time or another. Most people are too worried about themselves, too worried about the impression they are making, and too worried about what to say next to actually listen to what is being said.

In fact, most of us are too worried about not conveying enough about ourselves that we forget to listen to what the other person is really saying to us. We're too worried about the encounter being boring or uninteresting that we tend to fill it up with mindless chatter. Or, we're so used to talking on and on about ourselves (our favorite topic) that we forget there's someone else with us.

So, how do you go from being someone who has to tell the world about themselves to someone who actually listens? By taking the "I" out of the conversation.

The next time you're engaged in a conversation with someone and you start to use the word "I", stop yourself and readdress what you were about to say. Instead of saying; "I love it here," you could say something like: "This is a fantastic area. Are you enjoying yourself here?"

A good technique for creating rapport is by looking for things that can create a connection between you. When the person you're talking with (notice that I didn't say talking "to"?), says for example that they love the beach here or they had a great experience at a particular restaurant, you can say something like; "Me too, that place is great." It gives you both a sense of *commonality*, and is a clue that this maybe is someone with whom you have similar interests. And, with a little practice you can master this in no time.

—— FINISH LINE EXERCISE ——

▶ Find three ways to open up a conversation with someone.

Remember it's about progress not perfection. Once you have these three openers, find three ways to use them at least once a week.

Hello is often the best opener to begin a conversation. Also, always take note of your surroundings. Where you are and what the other person is doing can give you good material to begin a conversation.

<u>Examples:</u>

1. "May I ask what you ordered? That looks interesting."

2. "Someone recommended this place to me, have you been here before?"

3. "Excuse me, do you live in the area? I was looking for recommendations of a good place to eat."

4. "Can I ask how you like the book you're reading?"

The idea here is not to trick anyone or not be yourself. The exercise is meant to help you improve your level of comfort when approaching and speaking to new people.

Your goal is to develop this comfort muscle because the more opportunities you take to engage with other people, the more likely you are going to find someone who can help you with your goals.

—— FINISH LINE EXERCISE *continued* ——

The bigger your network becomes the more opportunities there will be that open many doors on your journey to the finish line.

People are curious by nature. When you get into a good conversational groove it's likely that they will inquire about you and ask what you do. Now is your opportunity.

REMEMBER: Conversation is a two-way street. The more you are interested in the other person the more they will be interested in you and your objectives.

At first, you will be nervous. Remember this tip: No one is judging you.

▶ **Approach at least one person a day for an entire week.**

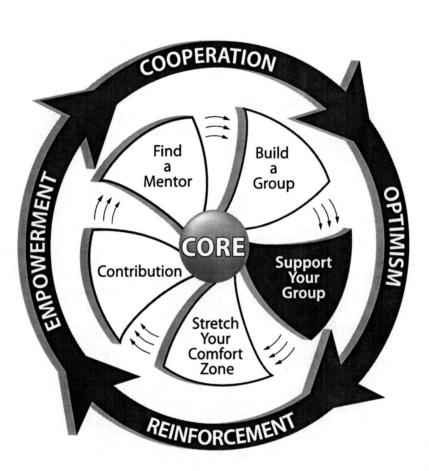

POWER PRINCIPLE

❷

SUPPORT YOUR GROUP

You must support and encourage the people in your group. Face to face contact on a regular basis is IMPORTANT. Do not use this CORE to dump your emotions onto. Constructive and positive feedback are key. Strengthen each member of your CORE. As they grow, you grow.

Keep in mind that support goes both ways. You too will need to encourage and motivate the others in your CORE to keep pushing forward towards their goals. Again, you don't want to enable them or mother/smother them. You're encouraging them to get to a point where they can jump out of the nest and fly with confidence. What an amazing thing for you and the people in your CORE to not only achieve anything you go after individually, but to help others reach their dreams as well. That is an incredible feeling.

Just imagine how good you'll feel knowing that another person had accomplished an amazing achievement in their life because you were there to support and encourage them?

Supporting others

"You can make more friends in two months by becoming interested in other people than you can in two years by trying to get other people interested in you."

- Dale Carnegie

When working with a group of people in your CORE your mission is to have them walk away with the feeling they're doing everything right and that they're on the right path. How do you do this? You want to give them useful, constructive feedback relating to something they shared with you that will give them clues about how to proceed. Anything you say that drives them forward will be useful to them. So how can you do this? When listening to someone, you want to encourage them. When someone calls, you need to focus the conversation on how to help them progress with their goal.

Keep in mind that as friends you will sometimes share things that you are worried, upset, sad, mad, angry, confused, frustrated, or bothered about. This is natural, but you will want to work on getting past this emotional state as soon as possible, because if you hang up the phone or end your conversation with these feelings and emotions hanging in the air, you are going to both or all walk away unsatisfied and disappointed. It's true that consoling another person can make you feel a little better, but mostly it leaves you drained and unfulfilled.

So you have two results you're going to come away with. One is that after your conversation with the other person, you want to make sure you have given them enough positive advice and feedback to drive them forward towards their goals. Your feedback is mission critical in moving their train to the next stop. The second result -

which is the most selfish and probably the most pleasurable of the two - is that when you hang up the phone or end the meeting with them, you too may feel fantastic because your words, counsel, advice, motivation, and direction has helped another person to feel great about where they are headed. You've just given them the proper ammo they needed to go out and tackle their objectives. Thanks to you, they are moving forward! That's a great feeling for anyone to have. How amazing is it that you've empowered another person to better their own life?

You're not there to instruct, give your opinion, criticize, or do anything to make the other person feel doubtful or self-conscious. That would make the session about you. Instead, your job is to add to their momentum to keep them positively moving forward.

Someone in my CORE group told me the other day that when he was helping me to figure out the next move for one of my projects, he actually figured out how to bulldoze through something that's been holding up *his* own progress.

He said two things occurred; when he was thinking of ways to help me with my project some of the ideas he came up with could also work for his own project. Secondly, as he was helping me with my goals, taking the focus off his own, suddenly, after being blocked for 6 months, he wasn't stuck anymore. He'd found clarity.

This same phenomenon happens time and again to people who are stuck and can't figure out the next necessary step to take.

People find that their creative blocks get unstuck at the oddest times:

- While watching a movie

- Playing a sport
- Reading for pleasure
- Doing charity work
- Going to lunch with a friend
- Listening to inspirational or improvement audios
- Stepping away from their project and focusing on something or someone else

In other words, all of them get clarity when doing something that was a complete distraction, which leads back to the main topic: **Supporting Your Group.**

By helping someone else who also is mission driven, three things happen:

1. It makes you want to really help them successfully reach their goal
2. It lifts any blocks that may be keeping you stuck
3. It hones your own clarity and focus

Why and how does this work? When we are too close to the inside of the circle it's often hard to see clearly what's around you. A better way to say this is; your vision of your GOAL can be very narrow when looking at it from ground level, but when you're high up in a tower looking down, you tend to gain greater perspective (insight).

Think of generals on a battlefield, observing the action from the hill above. Or the referee at a tennis match who sits in his chair high above. The lifeguard sitting in his tower. Can you imagine a forest ranger without the aid of a watch tower? Have you ever looked out from the top of the Empire State building, the Space Needle in Seattle, perhaps from the top of a mountain, or even the Eifel Tower? The perspective is quite different. Things suddenly seem a lot clearer. Type your home address in Google maps and look at it from a satellite view. Things will appear a lot different to you.

Taking your focus from the narrow to the expansive can be best done when first placing your focus on someone else.

Another benefit derived through supporting others in your group is that you want to keep them motivated and moving forward too. If they don't keep up to your level of progress or even slightly surpass you, you may find that you can stall out in your own progress by spending too much time dragging them along.

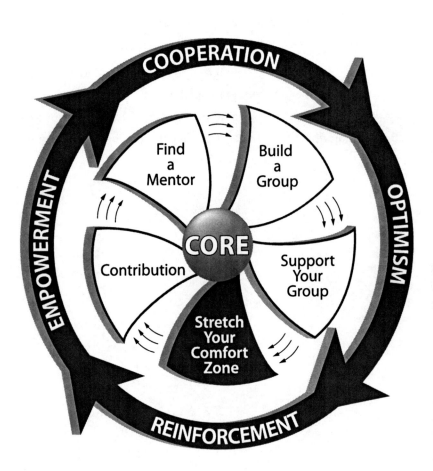

POWER PRINCIPLE

❸

STRETCH YOUR
COMFORT ZONE

Engage with someone new as often as possible. Ask questions. Get curious.
You MUST continually meet new people in order to see growth. Step out
of your box. You must continually put yourself in new situations. Challenge
your comfort level.

How To Reach Even Further

"You miss 100% of the shots you don't take."

   - Wayne Gretzky

Cell phones are an excellent way to be alone without feeling
lonely. But in reality, they are a band-aid or a crutch keeping you
from stretching your comfort zone and reaching out, meeting new
people, and expanding your CORE. Do not use escapisms to make
you feel complete. It will only last for a short time and eventually
leave you feeling empty. It's kind of like a sugar rush, it seems good
for a moment and then everything slows down. The key is to get out
and build an amazing network of supportive people in your life.

   I learned a great thing from Tim Ferriss, the author of *The 4-Hour
Workweek*. At first this lesson was hard for me. In fact, it was almost
painful. But now I can go for hours without having my cell phone
with me. I know some ex-smokers who went through the same thing

with cigarette withdrawal. At first it was very difficult for them to do, but eventually, (as I learned), they found the benefits that improved their life and direction. Once you can get to that place, it's freeing.

The easiest thing in life to do is to sit back and watch life zoom by you. It doesn't merely roll by, it flies! Ask someone who has just sat on the sidelines and finds that they're now in their 40s or 50s and regrets not having done more in their life. I'm sure you may know or have met someone like this before. Someone who is always looking back at the past, reminiscing about opportunities missed. Is that you? If so, this section is especially for you! It's not too late to get up and move! I'm more alive than ever, and I keep finding new and better ways to live life to the fullest. Challenges are exciting for me. Every encounter is a new adventure. If you tell me I can't do something, then watch as I get a big grin on my face and figure out how it can be done. And when I hit the top, I always find a new mountain to climb.

You may not need to live your life at such an intense level, but I can tell you it sure is fun. The point of this chapter is to get you to start living life a little bigger, and to give you the tools that will help you stretch yourself so you can make a difference in your life and the lives of others. Because interacting with other people is a big part of what life is really all about!

You may be someone who is more comfortable staying home, watching TiVo, and too tired to venture out into the world, or perhaps you're someone who does get out but remains isolated and hidden behind earplugs, a book, or newspaper. If so, then it's time to get you to stretch those muscles and give yourself a new outlook. This will be the foundation for revving up your motor and taking yourself to an entirely new place where things look and feel more alive to you.

You're going to start seeing the world in an entirely new way, unafraid to venture out. You may soon find you're actually excited to get out there and try new things.

The muscles I'm referring to are not your body muscles, but your social muscles. I want you to get out of your comfort zone. Try it.

When we engage in positive social activities, several things occur. You're taken out of your state of complacency and you begin to experience something outside of your normal realm. You begin to notice and absorb things around you and start to see life more acutely. Have you ever been in your little personal zone, walking with your headphones on or driving home from work, and suddenly you're surprised to be at your destination? We've all done it. What happened is you zoned out on life. Now you may be saying to yourself, "Big deal, it made the traffic go faster." True, but at what cost? Were there things you could have done to make that time more productive? Could you benefit by being more observant? More present? Did you take in the trees, the sunset, or the sky? Did you stop and breathe for a moment and acknowledge where you are in your life?

If you're someone who is content with staying in a safe, little world and never venture outside of your comfort zone, then this program is not for you. But if you're someone who's stuck in a rut or tired of being at home, bored, frustrated, and probably eating too much junk food, then you want to read on and see what great things are in store for you.

The key to living life is to engage with others. So the question becomes: How do you accomplish this? You start by interacting with other people. At first this may be something you really resist and that is foreign to you, but I can assure you that it can be learned and will eventually become enjoyable and even fun to do.

You may find this is easy and natural, or that it's a very challenging thing for you to do. You might be saying, "I can't talk to strangers. I'm terrified." And while it may be difficult for you in the beginning, what I want to do is to help get you to a point where it's not so overwhelming. Small steps are the key. Push yourself a little further every day so that it gets easier every time. Think of it like lifting weights. To build your muscles you either add more weights over time or do more repetitions. Both ways are effective in getting you the results you want.

When you learn or take on anything new it's going to feel strange and uncomfortable at first. When you start practicing *Power Principle Three* it's like exercising, taking a course, or driving for the first time. You're going to feel out of place. Just place your trust in the fact that as you walk through it again and again, you'll soon find it will become more familiar to you and less frightening.

So what kinds of questions can you ask someone? If you're looking for a store, you can ask for directions. You can mention that you like their shirt or shoes. Where did they purchase them? If you're in a store, ask if they'd ever tried the item they're about to buy. If they have, what did they like about it? Remember, your goal here is to build and stretch your comfort zone by interacting with new people. If you make friends as a result, that's a bonus!

What you don't want to do is to give unwarranted advice or your opinion if it's not solicited. Then, you would just come off as interfering and nosey. But when you ask another person about something they're doing, you show them you're interested and are looking to them for information and feedback.

We all love it when someone asks our opinion or advice. It makes us feel empowered and challenges us to really help the other person.

Keep that in mind when you talk to someone else. If you can ask their advice or opinion about something you give them a double benefit. You've given them the opportunity to help someone else, and you've subconsciously put them in a place of authority. Even if it's as simple as asking how they like that bread or tomato they're purchasing. Sometimes you'll be surprised at the doors a simple question can open.

Personally, I talk to everyone. I enjoy people and always notice them. Once I was in the produce section of the supermarket buying things for dinner because I'd just taken a cooking class and I wanted to put my new found skills to the test. I saw a lady who had this vegetable I'd never seen before and I asked her about it. It was so simple, and boy, did that question open up a can of conversation! She told me it was called a "chayote," which grows in Costa Rica and Mexico, and that it's delicious if prepared properly. The simplest way is to cut it into one inch dices, place it in a little olive oil, for a couple minutes, add chicken or vegetable stock, minced garlic and scallions. When tender add lime juice, lime zest, oregano, salt and pepper. Yum! She and her husband discovered it while traveling, and now it's one of their favorite foods. She described how it's so versatile that they use it in many dishes, and how they love to surprise their friends with it because they always ask what it is. Then she began to tell me the best ways to cook it, and how using a little lime juice brings out more of its flavor. She asked me what I like to cook and what I use and the two of us went on and on and on. I think we were even starting to get attention from the other shoppers who may have thought we had just started a 12-step meeting for vegetable lovers! I'm laughing to myself as I'm writing this just remembering the encounter. The point is, you'll never know what you're going to get from just a simple question until asked.

A great place to become comfortable talking with others is at your local coffee shop. When you frequent a place often, you create a comfortable environment for you to interact with others. It even has a built in bonus: You may find that the employees recognize you and welcome you back, and even remember your favorite coffee drink. And you may see other people there who are also regulars. You can acknowledge each other with a smile or a simple hello. They'll probably recognize you too. And as you continue to go there on a regular basis, you'll notice how quickly you get to know people there. Again, engage with them and ask them things: What are they drinking? Do they always order that drink? What do they think of a particular pastry? How are they enjoying their day? Do they live in the neighborhood? Where are they from?

So how do you approach someone? Have something to say! Your environment will offer plenty of things you can use to open a conversation with. If you're at the fragrance counter you can solicit someone's opinion of how a cologne or perfume complements you or has the opposite effect. If you're in a book store and someone is in the same section as you, you can ask for their advice on a particular topic or author. You'll find most people are intrigued when you ask for their opinion or advice, and are eager to help.

Finding something, anything to talk about will be unnatural for you at first. It will feel divisive to you in the beginning. And to a degree, it is. But it's a device that moves you forward, and it also enriches the lives of people you'll meet. The point here is to help you overcome this hurdle, to stretch your comfort zone, and to potentially meet new people who can enhance your life. Think about it like this... If you treat every encounter as a practice session where you're not concerned with the outcome or results, you then becoming more willing to take greater chances. So now that you are no longer outcome dependant, you now have the freedom and permission to venture into deeper waters and begin to challenge yourself. As you do this more and more you'll find it's easier to do and often fun to master.

Stretching your comfort zone is also about growth. And growth comes best when you challenge yourself. For example, taking a new course, hobby, or acquiring a new skill can all be great ways in which to stretch yourself. As I mentioned before, I didn't start mixed martial arts until much later on, but in taking up this new hobby, I did pursue a new challenge. Of course I'm not suggesting going after something as intense, unless it's what you desire, but taking a cooking course, running for the first time, or traveling to places you've never visited before, are all excellent ways to stretch yourself.

If you're single, get out of your rut and get into the dating game. If for no other reason, this teaches you a new set of skills; how to approach, engage, and talk with new people. And if done well, the outcome can be a bonus.

Let's talk about the word "rut" for a moment. A rut is a narrow or predictable way of life, a set of attitudes; a dreary or undeviating routine. Being in a rut means doing the same thing over and over until it's either no longer fulfilling or no longer satisfying.

While I'm not suggesting going out and skydiving tomorrow, again, unless that is your desire, I am saying that daily routine can lock you into a set of habits that don't offer any progress and two or five year later you find you're in the same place and have not gone any farther in your life.

Yes, it's hard to change, especially when your routine is so ingrained within you that you can't see a way out. You're consumed with just getting through your day, entirely filled with work and obligations, that you aren't able to see any new directions.

David was exactly like this. He was stuck in the same life routine for years and couldn't figure out how to extricate himself from work, paying his bills, trying to keep up, and simply making ends meet. Then one day something unexpected happened.

He was rushed to the hospital for a major surgery. And he was laid up for several weeks recovering from the surgery and getting his body back into full use. During that time he could not go to work, he got behind on his bills, and he was quickly falling behind on his obligations. But then, strangely enough, something else occurred.

He found that since he was already behind on these things he started looking outside of his box, his "rut" and started to explore and examine what else was out there in the world for him. Since he had to take it easy for a while, he began to notice other people and observed how they lived. He started talking to others and soon found himself taking courses on business and exploring new venture ideas. For the first time in a very long time he began to see new possibilities and changes in his life.

He thought about what he truly wanted, what his passions were and started taking courses how to help and assist others to improve their own lives. In no time, he became a coach and was assisting clients in getting out of their own stuck "ruts" and soon they too began seeing clearly for the first time.

Stretching your comfort zone is about breaking the "stuck" pattern you're in and thereby allowing you to see what else life has to offer. You may be someone who is meant to do more with your life. Take time to really think about and write down what your passions in life are. As Tony Robbins puts it, "what juices you?"

You can start by mixing up your regular routine. If you're a late riser, get up two hours earlier. Go for a walk or run. Write for thirty minutes. Go out and buy healthy groceries and prepare yourself a healthy breakfast. If you're already an early riser, stay up a little later and see if your creative juices get flowing at a different time.

Drive home using a different route. Talk to someone about helping you to change your clothing style. Go to one of those new fancy shaving places and get a shave by a gorgeous woman wielding a razor (it's scary but actually fun). Learn how to bake. Join a book club that has weekly meetings, find a local softball team, or even a basketball team at your gym. Start a cooking group in your neighborhood where once a week you all get together and do a theme meal.

You have plenty of options out there with which to stretch yourself. Find one or two that work best for you, that you can really see yourself doing more than only once and get yourself out there. Another great technique to really appreciate this is through *Power Principle number Four:* Contribution. This too is an amazing way to really stretch yourself. However, don't make it your only way. Try and choose a couple new things you can add to your life which can offer real progress and growth for you.

—— FINISH LINE EXERCISE *1 of 2* ——

▶ Here are three things to get you out of your comfort zone and into taking immediate action.

<u>Write down what you do:</u>

1. Pick one day and try something completely new to you. Go to the driving range, take a dance class, sign up to learn a new skill.

2. Meet three new people this week who could be potential candidates for your CORE.

3. Prepare one meal for yourself and/or your family. (You may need to go shopping for this one). If you already can cook, prepare a meal that's out of your comfort zone.

Why do this tasks and how will this help stretch your comfort zone?

Stretching your comfort zone is not simply about challenging your levels of comfort. It's also about learning to take action. The quicker you learn to take on a task the sooner you will attack the bigger challenges.

Most worthy goals and dreams are big. And most people will find ways to avoid beginning the journey. Different levels of overwhelm will begin to set in.

Learning to take instant action, you will begin to build momentum and hesitate less and less every time. Your mechanisms for procrastination and avoidance will diminish and your inner dialogue will became weaker.

TIP: Your new motto - Just do it, NOW!

—— FINISH LINE EXERCISE *2 of 2* ——

▶When you are thinking of approaching someone new, you should remember the 3-second rule: Approach the other person within 3 seconds of thinking about it. Don't hesitate beyond 3 seconds. If you wait any longer, you're more likely not to approach them.

1. Find someone to approach

2. Don't wait. 3-Seconds is the rule

3. Smile during the encounter

Bonus: Walk away knowing their first name

This rule is one of the most important rules when it comes to approach anxiety: The longer you wait before you walk up and talk to someone, the more your anxiety builds and builds.

You wait long enough and it is almost certain the approach will fail.

This comfort stretching exercise is not meant to keep you in uncomfortable situations. Instead its purpose is to help you to get through an uncomfortable situation so that you'll be more likely to go after the things you need for your life or business because you can now approach anyone.

Another aspect is that the more people who know about your goal or mission, the more likely you will meet or be introduced to the right person(s) who can help you on your journey.

The more willing you are to talk with people, the more opportunities will open up to you.

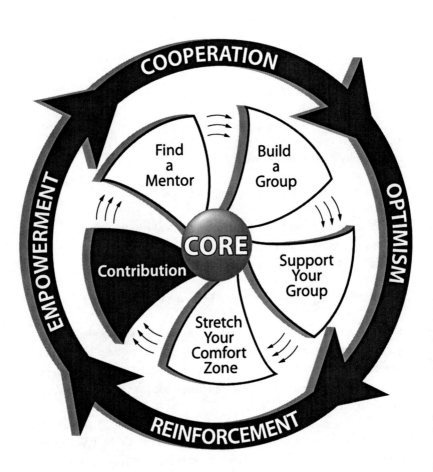

POWER PRINCIPLE

CONTRIBUTION

Give back. Find ways to volunteer. Help others in need. Contribute to the world. It elevates you, raising your self-esteem, and helps others to better themselves by your example. It can be as simple as helping someone with his or her groceries, opening a door for someone, or saying hello and thank you. It can be as big as helping a family in need, or donating your time and energy to a charitable organization. Preparing, serving, and handing out food or clothing. Building a home, etc.

Giving Back

"You can have everything in life you want if you'll just help enough other people get what they want."

   - Zig Ziglar

Volunteering will give you wings to soar. It's not just about helping others; it's about giving back. Amazing things happen when we contribute back to the world. When you're helping another person you cannot be on the bottom rung of the ladder. By contributing you actually elevate yourself. And if you think about it, volunteering is actually kind of selfish, because you get an equal (if not greater) benefit from the pleasure you experience when you help another person who really needs it. If you've ever held a door for someone, given food to a homeless person, handed someone an item they didn't realize they had dropped, rescued an animal, helped someone jump-start their car, or just said "hello" to someone who looked like they could use it. I'm sure you've experienced the incredible feelings you got from giving such a simple gesture.

Giving back and contributing does so much on so many levels, and does not take that much effort and time. Of course the more you do the greater you feel, and the more others benefit; but the goal here is to start anywhere with any amount of time or energy you can.

Volunteerism is a crucial part of this program to help you successfully reach your goals. The mission here is to get out of your own needs, put your ego aside, and be of service to the world in which you live. The objective is to ingrain yourself into the society in which you live and are a part of, and selflessly make an impact on others to better their own lives. Give them hope, a sense of self, purpose, or belonging - a reason to enjoy and appreciate their life in a pay it forward attitude. When you offer your services to another person, allowing them to feel like a part of society, you give them the spirit, drive, and energy to participate and offer their own services to the community and world in which they live.

No one wants to be in a position of needing help. Some just need the opportunity which enables them to get back on their feet and feel human again. To have a second chance at the life they want. Some may require more help than others, like the children of St. Jude's Foundation, Ronald McDonald House, or more recently, the victims of the tragedy in Haiti, Katrina survivors, and others.

As stated earlier, few people if given the opportunity want to be rescued. What they really want is the chance to get back on their feet and to a place where they can begin to take care of themselves again.

Helping others will give you such energy and confidence that anything you go after will seem easy to reach and within your sights. Volunteerism is a great way to put you in a frame of mind that empowers you in how you feel and it can change your outlook of the world. For some, it also creates a great source of inner strength.

Contribution is not just about volunteering, it can also be beneficial by showing someone wishing to accomplish their goal the ropes. In other words, showing them how you succeeded offers them the opportunity to succeed without having to endure the struggles you may have gone through.

There's plenty of room for people with goals similar to your own. Your contribution to them enables them to succeed while building stronger foundations for your group.

For the purpose of this Power Principle, any time you contribute something or volunteer, it must be done in person. Said differently, you cannot simply send money to a cause. While that's ultimately a good thing to do as well, the point of this exercise is to engage and interact with others. You're not going to get the maximum benefit from this Power Principle if you do everything remotely.

All of us were designed to engage with other human beings. Interacting with people benefits us by making us feel part of the larger community, part of life. Inspiration comes from socializing with another human being whom we may never have had the pleasure or even the desire to meet before. The satisfaction we receive from every encounter motivates us to do more. And it moves the world forward as well.

There is a company called TOMS Shoes that does an incredible thing. You may already have heard about them. For every pair of shoes they sell, they donate a pair to a needy child or family. The really big "wow" here is that they don't just send the shoes to some nameless child. They go in person and hand out hundreds and thousands of shoes. The rush of excited, happy, screaming children is enough to boost anyone's level of vitality. That feeling of engaging with another human being, who you've touched by the simplest of gestures, gives you back the greatest feeling a thousand times better than anything you've felt before. And children are so appreciative to receive the smallest of tokens. It cost the company very little to do this, and yet the reward is huge.

I remember when I volunteered my time at a dog park that I frequented with my dog, North. This was a lovely park in our neighborhood that had little funding and needed much improvement. So, along with others, I volunteered my time to spruce up the park by helping to scoop up poop, pick up trash, and get people water for their dogs. As it grew, we started to have fundraisers so we could get things like umbrellas for shade, a water fountain for the dogs, a fence to minimize problems, more trash cans, poop bags and scoopers, and to buy benches so we humans could enjoy the park, too. We put on events called *Bow Wow Ween* at Halloween, which became the hit of the community. Our attendance went from a hundred people to thousands in just a few short years. These were events where people could dress up their dogs in the most creative costumes and have celebrities judge the best, most inventive costumes. We had booths for food, and a celebrity charity auction that had some incredible donated items to help raise money for the park's improvement.

And when we didn't have the *Bow Wow Weens*, we had *Lemonade Fridays* where we sold lemonade to help raise additional funds. And even though we only asked for one dollar for a single glass of lemonade, people were so happy to help out and support the park that they would often donate twenty dollars; for a lemonade!

This gave me a great sense of contribution and participation in my community, and such a feeling of pride and joy. I also met many new friends, people whom I may never have met before, who are now my dearest and closest friends today. The funny thing is, if I met these people on the street I may never have become such close friends with them. It's true that while I like everyone on some level, some of our backgrounds would have made us less likely to hang out. (Some of us have different political views, or different value systems.) And while they are all great people, it's also true that as humans, we usually tend to gravitate towards people who are more like us. But my dog park friends, whom I never thought I would be friends with, are today some of the closest in my life and I think I have grown as a person by seeing the world through their eyes too.

Volunteerism and contributing are key to creating a life filled with feelings of success and accomplishment.

218

—— FINISH LINE EXERCISE ——

▶ Your mission is to do something every day that helps or benefits another person. Even the simple act of holding a door open or carrying someone's groceries to their car can be a wonderful thing. It's important to be present in the moment with that person, and to really engage with them. (This will also benefit you in the practice of stretching your comfort zone and increasing your network.) And while you don't have to become immediate friends with the person you're assisting, it may surprise you to learn what you get out of every encounter.

▶ Write down 10 thing you've done this week to contribute.

1.   6.

2.   7.

3.   8.

4.   9.

5.   10.

▶ Write down for 5 minutes how this made you feel:

—— FINISH LINE EXERCISE *continued* ——

DIG EVEN DEEPER:

Find one way you can volunteer your services (at least once a month) to an organization, charity or foundation whose mission it is to serve and help others.

Examples:

- Find a neighborhood mission or church where you can serve food, hand out clothing, or be of other service

- Call your local Ronald McDonald house and ask to volunteer your services cleaning rooms, stocking supplies, answering phones, etc.

- If you have a dog who's gentle and well behaved (and likes people) find out if you can have him/her work as a service dog at your local hospital, rehabilitation, or retirement home

TIP: Contribution to others builds great relationships, strengthens you socially, mentally, and builds esteem. When you put yourself out in society this way, others want to help you too in your mission.

The Ultimate Freedom

"You cannot do a kindness too soon, for you never know how soon it will be too late."

    - Ralph Waldo Emerson

What is giving back? Why do we do it and why do we need it? Volunteerism is something that should for the most part be altruistic. It's a selfless act that benefits and helps others. But it is much more than that. I don't know how many times over the years I've heard people say they do volunteer work because it makes them feel so much better about their own lives. It's kind of funny, but volunteering actually makes the giver feel great - sometimes, even better than the person receiving our gift. It elevates us to help another person. It makes the world seem more whole, more complete, more unified. It brings us together and unites us. Volunteering has so many benefits beyond just the person who is being helped directly. It gives purpose and unity to everyone involved.

When you assist another person by providing food, clothing, money, or time, you give them much-needed support. You also give them a sense of hope. You offer them a chance to feel like a whole human being. You allow them to regain their dignity and humanity. And with all of these great charitable gestures, you can't help but elevate and feel better about yourself.

It's an amazing but simple phenomenon. In fact, it's the best medicine when you are feeling down and alone, or feeling trapped and helpless. When you get a feeling of being lonely, it's often because you are isolating yourself and feeling like no one else is going through what you're going through, or that no one struggles like you do. You need to get out of your shell-of-self (or *selfish* mode) and go help someone in more need than you. In fact, you may find that you were not in a bad place after all. When you help another person, you start to really see exactly where you are in your own life and very often, you'll see that things aren't so bad. Helping another person is a gift you give yourself. It feels fantastic when you do something so simple yet gives so much reward.

Nowadays you hear of people giving back to the world in a variety of ways. Feeding and clothing the homeless. Feeding children in third-world countries that have no good source of nutrition, or the ability to grow healthy, sustainable foods. Finding new sources for potable, clean water for poor villagers to cook and clean with. Then there are the more creative people who take help to an entirely new level like Tom's Shoes.

However you decide to do it, the most important thing when it comes to giving back to the world is to simply get started.

The Importance Of A Thank You

"People will forget what you said, people will forget what you did, but people will never forget how you made them feel."

- Maya Angelou

The simplest of things can yield such big rewards. Have you considered the purpose of a "Thank you"? First, it's to acknowledge the person who has done a deed for you. Second, it's to show your appreciation. Third, it gives the other person a sense of satisfaction by their action, and a good feeling about themselves in return. When you thank someone, they feel good about having done something for you. They also want to experience that same good feeling again, either from you or the next person they give to. It also establishes a sense of community. One of the ways we build rapport with another person is by showing them our appreciation. It connects us. It shows we recognize and value others within our community, by thanking them for their time, their deed, or their thoughtfulness. By giving someone the simple acknowledgement of a "Thank you," you can fill someone with great pride.

What Does Giving Back Mean To You?

"Give the world your best and it may never be enough. Give the world your best anyway."

- Mother Teresa

Whenever I go to any place of business, whether it's a coffee shop, restaurant or store, I always say hello and ask the person on the other side of the counter how they're doing. Often they'll gloss over it and say, "What can I get you?" I repeat, "How are you doing today?" This usually will take them out of their robotic state and they'll respond, often adding a "Thank you for asking." Try this some time. You'll be amazed at the results.

Contribution is meant to either help another in need, help the world on a socio-ecological level, or to give added value to someone and make things better for them. We contribute in times of disaster, when things around us have become worsened, when someone or a group of people can no longer do and provide for themselves. We do this because we all want to be a part of our community. Because we as humans cannot live in a vacuum. And, because it's not all about taking. It's about leaving the world and your community better than you found it.

By the way, are you someone who is better at giving than receiving? If yes, raise your hand.

Now, do you think that successful people have trouble receiving? Probably not. They enjoy receiving and that's why they're successful, and they also know that since they enjoy giving, why rob someone else of the same opportunity to feel that same joy when they too are giving.

So if you are someone who desires and is willing to become successful, then you should also become someone who is great at receiving!

Reaching your goals too is a way of receiving.

Raise your hand if you're now a great(ful) receiver!

That's more like it.

— FINISH LINE EXERCISE —

▶ When you meet someone who doesn't have a smile, give them yours.

Your objective here is to:

▶ Smile at everyone

▶ Thank people for their time or thoughtfulness

▶ Ask someone how they are doing today

Always keep this humble frame:

1. You are not better than anyone else

2. You are not more deserving than anyone else

3. You are not owed more than anyone else

Instead reframe it as:

1. You can learn to become more successful

2. You have the ability to become more creative

3. You are someone who is more giving and generous to others

4. You are a smart person who can learn bigger and better ways to contribute to helping others

5. You can grow to become wealthier than ever before

6. You can choose that you want to be happier and share that state with everyone else

226

── **FINISH LINE EXERCISE** *continued* ──

Why? Because learning to have this standard gives others a goal by seeing how you do it. Doing things in this way sets the standard for how all of us as a society should live.

▶ Be kind and pay attention to those around you.

▶ Do not expect to be treated a particular way.

▶ Instead, earn that respect.

▶ Do not be rude to others.

▶ You never know their background, where they come from or what they have gone through.

▶ And, you may be missing a great opportunity.

Example: My book was offered to a book store I could never get into myself simply because I took the time to be kind and courteous to the person at Starbucks who happened to be great friends with the store owner. If you ever needed to get past a gatekeeper and reach a potential client, you know what I mean.

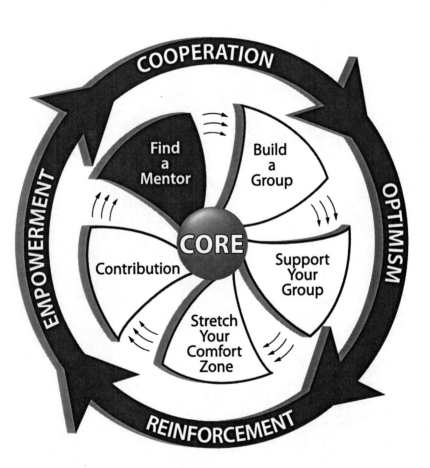

POWER PRINCIPLE

❺

FIND A MENTOR

Find people who play at a higher level. Someone you aspire to be like. Find someone who challenges you to better yourself. A mentor is someone who has gone through the steps and is able to offer experience, wisdom, and insights, valuable to your own goals and objectives.

Why You Need A Mentor

"If I have seen further it is by standing on the shoulders of giants."

- Sir Isaac Newton

If you look at any highly successful person, you will almost always find a mentor behind them. It's really hard to imagine that some people don't have mentors. Yet it's one important way we grow as people. As a society, we often tend to put people of celebrity on a pedestal. In fact, it almost seems as if some famous people were just born awesome when in fact, the truth is that it took many setbacks and failures before they achieved greatness.

Napoleon Hill had Andrew Carnegie. As did Charles Schwab. Confucius had Lao Tzu. Gandhi had Dadabhai Naoroji. Warren Buffet had Ben Graham. Mother Teresa's mentor was Father Michael van der Peet. Michael Jordan had Phil Jackson. Tony Robbins had Jim Rohn. And the list goes on and on.

First of all, what is a mentor, and how can you recognize a good mentor for you? Before we go deeper, it's important to understand that a mentor is not necessarily someone famous. The criteria for an amazing mentor is someone who has successfully achieved something that you too are looking to become successful at. A mentor is someone in your life who is living life at a higher lever than you currently are, who advises you on how you too can achieve your objectives. A mentor has achieved goals that are often similar to yours. They are fulfilling their own goals and dreams, and accomplishing things that others often envy or desire. The best mentors resonate with you, and they seem to have an understanding about which path leads you to getting the best results.

When we think of successful people, we often think of people in the media like Donald Trump, who is a Real Estate guru. Bill Gates and Steve Jobs have the technology world at their fingertips. Richard Branson seems to go after everything he touches with vigor and success. And so do Martha Stewart and Oprah Winfrey. You want to be like that. You may look at someone like George Clooney or Naomi Watts, and wonder how it became all so easy for them. How did they get so lucky? What was the secret to their success?

When you were a child, you started to watch and emulate the people you wanted to be more like. You might have pretended you were a superhero, or a rock star, or a ballerina, a baseball player, or favorite celebrity, hoping that by copying them and their style you might stumble upon the secrets that made them the stars they are today.

But there is another aspect to a great mentor. They are people who can guide and direct you towards the right path. They give you an understanding of the steps necessary to reach your goals. They give you the sense that your dream can be realized, they reinforce the best in you and mold your strengths to allow you to meet your own goals.

Here is a checklist you can use to help you find the right Mentor:

Experienced: In this, age is not a necessary factor, but you want someone who has knowledge and experience in your field.

Character: This should be someone you respect and admire since it is they who will be coaching and guiding you. Preferably someone with good moral standing.

Similar Goals: Your mentor should be someone who is on a similar path or has already gone through what you have in front of you.

Availability: Your mentor needs to have time for you. If not, what's the point? However, you should also respect their time and not abuse this privilege.

Open-minded: We all learn and grow at a different pace. If your mentor is someone who is conscious of this it will allow you to progress in a way that you need to progress.

Positive: This one should be obvious. You don't want to choose someone who has disdain for everything and carries a negative outlook on everything they encounter. Their attitude, negative or positive, is bound to influence you.

Focus: Starting any goal can be overwhelming. A mentor can help direct you to what might be the most important point in terms of starting towards reaching your objectives.

Modeling

"If your actions inspire others to dream more, learn more, do more and become more, you are a leader."

    - John Quincy Adams

The difference between modeling and emulating someone is that emulation can incorporate mimicking what someone has - not necessarily what they do. When someone observes Michael Jordan or Shaquille O'Neal and sees them owning several houses and multiple cars and they too want those perks of success, that person is most likely wanting to emulate them.

Modeling someone involves getting inside the behaviors, thoughts, and attitudes that drove them towards their success in the first place.

When you're looking for a mentor, seek to get insights into the methods, mindsets and processes they used to achieve their successes and the steps that got them where they are so you can duplicate their model. While there's nothing wrong with wanting some of the things in life that they possess, your goal here is not necessarily to be able to buy the same car they have, but how to duplicate the success that *allowed* them to have the financial resources and freedoms they enjoy.

Early in my life I noticed that people who were not financially or economically set were driving Mercedes and other new cars. When I asked my mother about this, she told me that anyone could purchase something desirable, but it didn't mean they had the financial security to maintain a complete lifestyle that allowed for them to have the other things necessary in their lives to be financially secure. These same people still shopped with coupons and were probably in debt, had too many credit cards and lived hand to mouth day-to-day. A lot of people today are still doing this, and are just learning now how using credit has ultimately put them into a difficult financial situation.

If you want material possessions, you can get those now. But if you want to model and duplicate the successes of the top people and sustain that level of success, then you have to get into their thinking processes and learn how they map out their strategies towards reaching their goals.

Where Do You Find A Mentor?

"When the student is ready, the teacher will appear."

\- Buddhist Proverb

Mentors come in all shapes and sizes. You might find that you have more than one mentor for the various areas of your life. This is common. Just like with your CORE, keep in mind that you should not use your mentor to dump your emotions onto. This is not productive and not the purpose of having a mentor. Sometimes a mentor can be someone you've met at a coffee shop who has gone through a situation similar to your own. They have experience in achieving what has now become your own goal. And their knowledge and experience can benefit you by showing you shortcuts around the pitfalls that will inevitably arise as you pursue your dreams. They often have the wisdom, experience, and contacts that can help rocket you towards the finish line.

If you desire to become an architect, for example, you may seek out the advice of someone who presently works for an architectural firm. It would make sense to seek them out and ask for their advice and counsel.

Again, I don't know how many countless people I meet who've become my mentors simply by speaking with them in a casual environment such as Starbucks.

Another great place to find a like-minded mentor is through seminars. Often when you attend a live seminar, one of the improvement techniques is to do an exercise they assign you to do with someone you haven't met or spoken with before. This exercise is meant to challenge and stretch you out of your complacency, and another benefit is that it also introduces new and really great people into your life. Of course there will be some people you meet who are presently at your level, but others you encounter may be just the ticket you need. Both can benefit you. Or you may find that you meet someone who has the ability as well as the capability to take you and guide you through to the next level on your journey. There is also a secondary benefit to meeting with and talking to as many new people as you can during this seminar time. While you may not meet your mentor during the event, there is a good chance that someone you do meet will have a friend or connection in their life they want to introduce you to who can potentially become a great mentor for you. This has happened to me personally more times than I can count.

The phrase; "When the student is ready..." means that you have to put yourself into a position where you can let as many people as possible know about your goal to find a mentor. And the more specific you are about what your needs are in having a mentor; the more likely it is that you will be put in touch with the right person. Asking is a huge part of finding the right mentor for you.

What you don't want to do is to find a mentor because you think they will hand-hold you through the process. They are not there to rescue you and it is not their desire. Instead, a great mentor is someone who wants to work with a person who already has real passion and vision about their direction in life and needs some vital tools and guidance to get there. They are not there as a counselor, they are there to offer their own experiences and resources to give you forward momentum. However, a Life-coach is an excellent source if you are someone in need of counseling and figuring out your direction and how to focus on finding your goal.

Tim Ferriss, author of The 4-Hour Workweek suggests finding the specific person you want as a mentor and contacting them. Now I know you may be thinking; "Right, I'm just going to call him or her and they are going to drop everything to help me." Well yes, sometimes. In fact, I contacted Tim Ferriss. It didn't go as I'd hoped but only because as it turned out he was on a major deadline and didn't have time for anything more added to his plate at that particular time. On the other hand, I've contacted many others who have now become my mentors and it has worked out brilliantly.

It may take more than one time to get in touch with them. Sometimes you may have to learn patience. But persistence does pay off as long as it's done in a friendly, non-harassing way that also won't make the person you are seeking out as a mentor feel like they've made the biggest mistake by helping you. In other words, don't overwhelm them with a ton of needs and requests. Use their time and your time with them wisely, sparingly. But don't feel you need to walk on eggshells either. You are someone who has a goal and you are seeking the counsel and advice of someone more experienced who has great insights on how to make your journey a successful one. So use your time with this person wisely. You won't necessarily be going to the movies together and hanging out all the time, but you do want to contact them with questions that are specific and focused, that by having the answers, will help to drive you forward towards the finish line. Said a different way, you want to make sure that the time spent with your mentor is used to progress you forward. It should not be used as a cool story because you hung out with a famous person. Think how you'd want to be treated if you were someone's mentor.

Again, having a specific goal in mind, working out your elevator pitch, then being willing to ask as many people as you can, who they think might be the best mentor to help you reach your goal or objective, is a great formula for finding a meeting the right mentor for you.

Also, please keep in mind this partnering is a two-way street. Just because someone has some of the skills or tools you need and are looking to learn from and incorporate into your own skill set, does not mean everyone will be a good match for you. You have to make sure that the person you choose for a mentor doesn't use up or waste too much of your own precious time.

To better illustrate this, when an actor seeks representation through finding an agent or manager, they are often so concerned about getting hired themselves, that they forget that they too are deciding if this is the best person to have representing them. In other words, the audition process should be a two-way street. You need to make sure the other person is as good a fit for you as you are for them. Please always keep in mind that this is *your project, your goal,* and that you are the one seeking help and advice. Choose your mentor wisely.

What Having A Mentor Will Do For You

"Practice isn't the thing you do once you're good. It's the thing you do that makes you good."

　　- Malcolm Gladwell (Outliers)

On so many levels you'll immediately reap several benefits from having a mentor. If you've ever had a Life Coach or you know what they are, you know there is a benefit to checking in with another individual. The main drawback to working with a Life Coach can sometimes be the feeling you have to turn in homework, and after a while some people begin to question having to pay for someone to coach them, who is sometimes not in the same field as you. But if you have the financial resources and you're someone who benefits from reporting your progress to a trained professional, then a Life Coach may benefit you.

However, a Life Coach is not a substitute for your CORE. You can think of a Life Coach like a trainer in the gym who guides you and tweaks your performance so you get better and better results as you work toward your goal. Just like with a mentor or a member of your CORE, you'll want to make sure that the coach you choose is a match for you.

Choosing the right coach can mean the difference between resenting paying someone who's ineffective for you, and working with someone who helps you exceed your goals and gives you more than your money's worth.

In contrast to a Life Coach, the way a mentor works is more like a member of your CORE. He is typically someone who has experience within the field or goal you're pursuing. You are continuing on your path to progress while getting positive feedback from your mentor. Your mentor assures you that you are on the right course by showing you the necessary steps. Another benefit of having a mentor is that you can often use their accomplishments as a guideline to your own progress. Most likely, you won't get that same benefit through a Life Coach as you will from a great mentor.

And quite often, you'll find that your mentor will have advice, contacts, and methods you can use to streamline your progress. Finding the right mentor can give you direction and save you many hours (or sometimes years) in reaching your goal. He or she can open doors that can elevate and drive you forward. Their knowledge, connections, and experience can often be the difference you need in meeting the high objectives you set for yourself.

Finding a mentor is a key element toward successfully completing what you start. The goal here is to help you learn a new process and get rid of the old ones that were holding you back. A mentor can help you create a path through the trees that wasn't there before, saving you hundreds of hours of energy you would have spent figuring things out.

Within all the *Power Principles* is the underlying key of forward movement and continuing to climb the ladder. Of all the *Power Principles*, number Five: Finding a Mentor is the one that will really help you see how to climb the ladder of success. A mentor with experience and know-how will not only accelerate the learning curve, he or she will keep you on the right path and tell you the best shoes to wear for the journey.

What's A "Mini-Mentor," And Why Do I Want One?

"When you really lock in with a mentor, you start to understand the meaning behind their words."

- J.D. (Scrubs)

"I'm, I'm just happy you haven't messed up yet today."

- Dr. Cox (Scrubs)

Have you ever had some expert help in completing a task or a project that made it possible for you to complete it faster and better than you expected? If you have, then you've experienced some benefits of having what I call a "Mini-Mentor" on your side.

A Mini-Mentor is someone who can be helpful for the duration of a particular task or project. It may be someone you use again and again for their advice and expertise, even if they don't stay in your life as one of your primary mentors. If you're acquiring a new skill like writing a book, or learning a new routine in the gym, or finding an agent (if you're an actor), or where the best place to buy the right plants to landscape your yard is, you may seek out the advice of a Mini-Mentor to help you complete your goal. They might be someone who sticks by you as you complete your project and/or learning curve, or they may be someone whom you refer to again and again throughout your life. Remember that part of your goal here is to expand your network, build your community, and strengthen your CORE. Mini-Mentors can give you many benefits towards this as well.

When writing my first book there was a lot I didn't know and therefore wasn't able to prepare for. For the preparation of this book

I started asking a lot of people a lot of questions. I met someone who it turned out had a great deal of knowledge about publishing a book. Everything from getting an ISBN number, where to find a great cover designer, finding a good editor, and how to best secure great testimonials. He also walked me through the various types of distribution that were available and how to select the right one for me.

Before approaching a potential Mini-Mentor, you need to identify what you hope to gain from a mentoring relationship and what type of a mentor is best for helping you meet your objectives. Start by identifying your short-term goals. Where do you see yourself heading? What knowledge, skills, and abilities will you need to get there? What key experiences could a Mini-Mentor provide that would benefit you most? Answers to these questions will help you identify the type of Mini-Mentor that is right for you. For example, depending on your goals, you may want to seek a high-ranking executive whose career path you would like to learn from. Or you may want a mentor closer to your level of experience, but who you feel could help you in very specific areas of growth and knowledge.

Much of the responsibility for initiating a mini-mentor relationship is going to be on you. You need to have the self-confidence to approach a potential mentor and effectively present the merits of a mini-mentoring relationship. Once you have found an appropriate individual, share your short-term goals, your accomplishments, and your major developmental needs and objectives as long as the area of endeavor you're pursuing is congruent to what they presently do. Your potential Mini-Mentor needs to know if he or she will be able to help you acquire the skills or competencies you want to develop. Be completely honest in your explanation of why you want a Mini-Mentor and why you are asking this particular individual.

— Framework —

The tools of the *5 Power Principles* using the Foundation of CORE

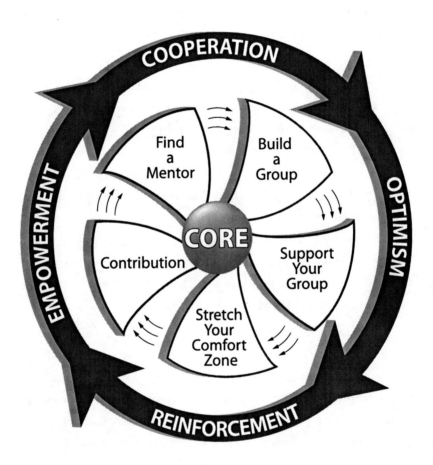

Part 4 —
Bringing It All Together

Finishing What You Start

"Success doesn't come to you, you go to it."

   - Marva Collins

This entire book has been geared towards helping you *Finish What You Start*. By now you should have clarity in terms of the direction you want to go. You should already have a goal or objective that you want to reach. Life is not going to stroll by you; it's going to fly past. Unless you take control and go after it. Earlier in this book we looked at Brian Tracy's "Eat That Frog" mentality, where you tackle the biggest, hardest project first. After some exercises we did earlier on in the book, where we practiced a few smaller Task Completion exercises, you should now be in the frame of mind where your accomplishments are your rewards. Now you're ready to go to the next level and really tackle the bigger objectives in your life.

Bringing this all together to create the most effective results you will need to incorporate equal parts of all five of the *Power Principles* into your life. You may think it's more beneficial for them to concentrate primarily on Power Principle number Five by finding a mentor. However, putting too much emphasis on one Power Principle while neglecting the other four will leave you lacking. You may also find that it is harder to attract the right mentor as he or she may pick up on the fact that you don't have all the necessary areas of your life running at peak level. That someone may feel that you're not quite ready to be seeking out a mentor at this time.

This, of course, is just an illustration. The point is that when you incorporate all five of the *Power Principles* into your life, the energy and drive you exhibit will become attractors for the right people to come into your life. Like attracts like, and when someone is in tune with the world around them, we sense their similar energy.

When you're creating a group of people who are supporting you in positive ways, this creates momentum in your life and you want to *do* even more. One way to create this momentum is assisting and supporting others as they do for you. This is a natural next step. As you have more positive results, you gain courage and strength in your choices. From there, you'll naturally want to try new things and stretch your comfort levels. When you find that the challenge of stretching yourself is actually something you look forward to, you are then open to seeing the world around you with more clarity and you'll want to give back and support that world. This, of course, will elevate you even further. And when you are elevated to a higher level, you feel empowered and want to go even farther in your goals.

From here, the next and last natural step for you to take is to find a mentor who can guide, challenge, craft, and hone your talents using the skills and experience he or she has successfully used to create the amazing life they now enjoy.

In this way, using all the *Power Principles* together will only drive you towards creating unstoppable success in your life, all the time, every time. This is the best way to empower yourself. This gives you the ability to improve your life, promote your growth, and it gives you more freedom to go after larger challenges and goals.

Finish What You Start is *really* about getting started, through having an objective, making a decision towards reaching it, taking an action to begin, and constant forward movement towards your goal. The steps I've outlined in the book will give you the tools to get started and keep the momentum going.

— FINISH LINE EXERCISE —

▶ Get out a piece of paper and create a graph or chart that you can look at every day.

1. On this piece of paper list six goals you've set for yourself and want to accomplish. They can be big or small.

2. Set a time frame for each and be SPECIFIC! The more detailed you are the more your mind will set its sites on getting there.

3. Draw a progression level indicator (like a thermometer) showing every new level of progress you've achieved.

4. Make sure there's a space between each goal, so your eyes can absorb each one.

5. If you have images or photos of what you want to achieve, you can place them next to each task to reinforce them. Doing this will make them more real. And, like any memory game, using an image will help it stick with you longer.

TIP: Make a point to look at this every day. If you place it somewhere that you seldom traffic or visit, the less likely it is that you will reach those goals. Check in every day for accountability and so you can see how quickly you are reaching the finish line.

Enjoying Your Alone Time - The Magnificent Self

"Knowing others is intelligence; knowing yourself is true wisdom. Mastering others is strength; mastering yourself is true power. If you realize that you have enough, you are truly rich."

- Tao Te Ching

One of the primary reasons why we drop out of any self-help or self-improvement program, whether it is dieting and weight loss, fitness, or learning a new skill, is that too often we feel alone as we're working towards our goals. In the beginning, we attack our new objective with vigor and enthusiasm. At first, it seems so close you can almost taste it. So you make a time commitment towards reaching it every day. You put out your running shoes or the things needed for that task at hand the night before so you can immediately jump right in and get to it first thing in the morning. And for several weeks or months you actually accelerate at your task, seeing improvements along the way and see the target is in your crosshairs.

But after a while, the enthusiasm begins to fade and you look for ways to miss a couple of sessions. Or you were exhausted because work was too hard that day or the kids are too demanding, or life gets in the way. But when you started, none of this mattered. You committed to making sure that none of these typical excuses would get you off track. Do you remember feeling that way? So what changed?

Fundamentally it comes down to the same reason every time. It's not that you're a loser or that you aren't good enough, strong enough, powerful enough, worthy enough, smart enough, or capable enough.

It's just the simple fact that doing anything alone for any sustainable amount of time eventually becomes boring. You lose the drive and enthusiasm you once had. It happens to us all.

It's not your fault. But it's a problem that's inherently built into anything we do alone. When you go to the gym, it's usually alone. When you go to a Weight Watchers meeting, you typically go alone, even though you may see a group of people there you recognize. When you take a new course of any kind, very often you show up there alone. It's why some people hate cooking at home alone, or going to a restaurant alone, or to the movies alone. It's not as fun or as powerful an event as when you share the experience with someone. It's why we enjoy going out to a concert or movie with someone else so we can share the experience together. It unites us, builds rapport, and creates a bond between us. There are some people who've simply come to the false realization that they will always be alone and do cook for themselves or bring a book when they go out for a meal, but they often don't experience the same excitement and passion of life when they do these things. Typically this can happen in a large city like New York, Chicago, Boston, or Los Angeles where there are hundreds of people all around, yet they still feel alone. They do things alone because it's better than the alternative, but really what they desire is a companion to share the experience with.

By now, you should be able to see how the group can actually strengthen and improve the confidence of the *self*.

One of the primary benefits of the 5 *Power Principles* is the ability to enjoy the benefits of your "alone time." You'll actually maximize your time and energy, enjoying the time you have to be alone. Why? Because you'll see alone time as a reward or benefit, or a way to relax and unwind. This may seem counterintuitive, but the value and momentum you get from the group you build along with the richness of having a fulfilling social life will actually make you look forward to your alone time.

The CORE that you'll build will give you an amazing sense of yourself and such a sense of empowerment that when those times arise that you are alone, you'll feel as if you're surfing on top of the wave and not getting swallowed up in the undertow. Your CORE is the foundation through which you'll become a stronger individual. Its purpose is not to make you dependent on others for your successes, but to give you incredible energy and confidence to complete everything you take on by yourself. Ultimately, you won't feel alone any longer. You will have the power of your CORE behind you, encouraging you to push forward and complete the task.

Success Is Alchemy

"No one can make you feel inferior without your consent."

- Eleanor Roosevelt

From this moment forward you need to be passionate AND excited about what you do. If you want to be successful, passion is going to be the driving force that keeps you going. Remember, it's motivation that GETS you going, and passion that KEEPS you going strong.

Always make sure that once you have a clear idea of what your *passionate* goal is, that you write it down and place it somewhere you can see it every day. Setting goals you can look at each and every day will help you to stay focused and become consciously and subconsciously accountable to reaching your objectives. It will be the key to helping you to stay on track.

Reflect. Every day, take some time to think about what you want and where you're headed. Did you know that the main difference between successful people and ordinary people is the fact that successful people think about what they want all the time? The more you think about what you want, the more you are going to condition it into your subconscious mind. This is what you want because once the idea of achieving your goals has been conditioned into your subconscious, you'll begin do things towards reaching your goals automatically. The process of moving towards the finish line, where you want to be in your life will become an automatic part of your routine.

Choose what you think about. Make an effort to really see the results of already having achieved your goal and how exciting it will be to reach your objective. Every day, continue thinking about what you want all the time.

If you aren't committed, no one else will be either. If you're not committed, you'll never produce the results you want in your life. It is only when you're fully committed to achieve what you want for your life that you'll stay on target and do more empowering things to make your dreams reality.

Successful people are committed toward their dreams and goals. And so are you. It is your commitment that will help you breakthrough all the difficulties and obstacles in your life. It is your focus and dedication that will help you solve all the problems you meet while driving you forward.

Action is the driving force. You need to take action to produce the results you want in your life. This is where most people fail and miss out on what it takes to achieve what they want most in life. It's up to you to do something to make your DREAMS come true. What you learn here is not going to change your life. Taking action will. Learning and applying action to your life will change you. You'll never be the same person again.

Enjoy your life. Reward yourself by taking some rest or by having fun. It's been shown that if you want to be more productive, you must keep a refreshed mind. You must rest and relax and enjoy your life or the rest means nothing. It's important to make time for recreation. Why? Typically when we exercise a specific set of muscles in the gym, the rule of thumb for the best results is to have a day or two of rest. That is why recreation, or if we break it apart, RE-CREATION is so vital to our success. Of course, there will be times you'll get stressed and pressured by situations that have deadlines. And sometimes it will seem like you'll fail to get the results you want no matter how hard you try. When faced with this situation, take some time to rest and go play and RE-CREATE yourself. If you keep on going without rest, you're going to ultimately break down in the end. So live a balanced life with both work and play. Go to lunch with friends. Go see a funny movie. Go for a drive. Whatever. If you can learn to unwind, you'll have the mind and energy to truly be successful.

Contribution is huge. One of the greatest feelings of success is the feeling of self-esteem. Do you know that you can boost your level of self-esteem and confidence by helping others? You need to go out and help others. People who are in need. People who can learn from your experience or benefit from your viewpoint. The key is to contribute to people around you. You want to train your mind to cultivate the spirit of community, togetherness, and contribution. You want to feel that you're part of this big world and you're doing something to help to make others lives better. If you want others to treat you good, treat them good first. If you want others to treat you great, be a great person. Give, then give some more.

Are you grateful yet? I hope so. Be thankful for who you are. Why? Because you've been given the gift of becoming someone who can do anything you set your mind to and change your life for the better. You are, and always have been in control of your destiny. The choice is yours. You can choose to lie in bed and sleep all day, or make some tough decisions to change your life any way you want. If you think that you're unlucky or not as good or gifted as others, think again. There are many people who are worse off than you who dream big about the very opportunities you have right now to change their own lives. You, on the other hand, have the power to do so right now. Be thankful and adopt the habit of being grateful within your life.

Successful people work very hard and practice until they come out on top. They are always learning, growing, changing, and evolving. Their outcome is only the tip of the iceberg; it is only the 10%, the rewards, or fruits of their labor that the rest of us see. The remainder, the 90%, is preparation, hard work, effort, and planning to invest in themselves, that gave them their amazing successes.

When they focus on a goal or objective the rest of the world disappears until they reach the finish line. All their attention and all their resources work together for their goal. These successful people don't let themselves get overwhelmed by "urgent, non-important" issues that could pull them off their course. And, they are constantly prioritizing.

They also have passion about everything they do. They like and actually enjoy what they do. Any way you put it, their hard work is a pleasure and a must for them because they know the reward is even more pleasurable.

Become childlike again. Successful people always want to know more. They want to learn more. The questions they most frequently ask are not "What? When? Who?" but rather "Why? Or How?" The best way to repeat a successful action is to know why it was successful and how it generated attraction and recognition. Become curious and don't be afraid to feel the clay between your fingers, and find out how many ways there is to mold it into the life of your dreams.

Help others. Be a generous, giving spirit. Have you noticed how many people like and want to emulate successful people? It's because their way of living resonates with others. They are experts at creating rapport. They are empathic, and people like and feel good around them. That is because of their ever improving abilities to listen and learn from the world.

Be responsible in your actions and deeds. When something happens, don't waste time searching for whose to blame. Instead, move on to finding out what needs to be done next. Don't search for reasons to complain and don't look for pity. Heeding this advice, you will become stronger in mind and spirit. You'll attract healthier more successful people into your life, and you'll feel infinitely freer than you've ever felt at any time before.

Always strive to be someone who is constantly learning and developing. Successful people are always striving to work on themselves. They change with the times and learn from the past.

Laugh at yourself, Laugh at the world. Appreciate humor. Live in the spirit of joy and relaxation.

Get more creative than you are now. Successful people always strive to think out of the box; searching for new and better ways to do things. They always strive to do more, yet they learn to be flexible. Be someone who knows how to spot opportunities and change with them. This will create more joy, satisfaction, and willingness to take greater risk in your life. Always work to be positive. Think Success, not Failure. Be aware of when you walk into a negative environment and immediately change that pattern for the better.

Your belief that you can accomplish your goals has to be unwavering. The moment you say to yourself "I can't...", then you won't. Never say "I can't". Time-to-time your attitude may waiver. This is ok, but you must not stay in that mental state. Positive things will only happen to positive people.

Self confidence is the difference between feeling unstoppable and feeling like you can't make it. It's your own perception that has enormous impact on how others will perceive you. The more self confident you are, the more likely it is you'll succeed.

Confidence That Sticks

"Success leaves clues."

- Jim Rohn

Confidence comes out of repeated experience and positive results. Confidence builds daring, it enhances character and opens one up to see farther than before, because through confidence we can look beyond our immediate limitations and seek new adventures outside our comfort zone. Confidence grows from habit that has been infused with success. It's nurtured through routine. On the smallest level we are so confident that we can properly tie our shoelaces, that we may not even glance at our hands tying the knot. As a toddler we wobble when first learning to walk. As an adult, we don't even think about it. On a larger scale, our confidence comes through repeated positive results whether it's in closing a business deal or sale, going to the gym and working out regularly, or writing a third and fourth novel or script. To build confidence, build a routine.

Build the habit of writing out the next day's tasks the evening before. You will wake with a conscious purpose and a clear idea of how best to handle the tasks in front of you. Check off each completed task as you go through the list. This will give you a greater sense of accomplishment. It will also build within you the tools for streamlining the process. When you chart your tasks out the evening before you begin to brainstorm the best, most effective way to tackle every task. If these are errands, you may even map out the most efficient route in which to travel. Make a point to do this every day and your drive towards success will grow stronger and more powerful.

When writing out your goals, be as thorough and complete as possible. Detail all the steps necessary in order to complete every goal with success. Do not worry about how big or small your goal or project is. Writing the details and steps down are necessary to see it through to completion. This will also build a *finish what you start* foundation within you which you'll notice begins to level the playing field and gives everyone at any level the habits of someone who is successful.

E. E. Cummings once said "The most wasted of all days is one without laughter." To this point, never be too busy to laugh, or too serious to smile. Instead, surround yourself with fun people and don't get caught up in your own sense of importance.

Slow down for just a moment, look around you, and take the time to appreciate ordinary events, life will become instantly more enjoyable. Always strive to connect with people. In so many ways, it is our relationships with people that offers us the most happiness in life. And by all means, keep learning. There is an amazing link between learning and happiness. Given this, there is no excuse not to be stimulating your brain and learning something new each day. My favorite way to find time for learning is to make the most of the commute to and from work. Books on CD and podcasts are excellent for this purpose.

Pay attention to both your mornings and your nights. Are the mornings a mad rush for you to get out the door? Do you switch off the TV at night and go straight to bed? There are profound benefits from establishing a routine in the morning and evening. For example, in the morning you may choose to wake up two hours earlier, as Brian Tracy suggests, and spend the time working on yourself, thinking about the day ahead of you, preparing. Also, writing or exercising are excellent ways to start your day. In the evening, consider spending some time just before bed reviewing your day or in reflective meditation.

And most of all enjoy your successes. Why not take a moment to acknowledge what you've achieved? Then share the experience with someone else in your CORE.

You and I are done for now. But YOU are just beginning. Let's see what happens from here. As the Dr. Seuss title says; —Oh the places You'll go!

About The Author

Craig has worked as a high-level Personal Assistant for 15 years for some of the top CEOs of major corporations, Entrepreneurs, Venture Capitalist, top Producers, Directors, A-list actors, Grammy winning performers, and heads of major movie studios.

He was chosen by Celeb Staff Magazine in 2009 as one of the Best of the Best Personal Assistants and ranked among the top in elite household and business staffing. His first book, The Celebrity Assistant's Handbook is considered to be an authoritative nuts and bolts guide for the industry.

He's been a speaker for several years and has recently begun speaking at seminars through his company the Reach Now Institute based on his new book *Finish What You Start: Unlocking the Success Secrets of the Top 1%.*

Craig has worked for several years as a trained Crisis Intervention Counselor and has logged hundreds of hours counseling, and working with people on how to improve their lives to make a difference.

His life goal is to create his foundation he calls the *Theophilus North Foundation*, named after his cherished Aussie Shepherd, whose focus will be to enable third-world children to attend school, to feed and clothe them, to make sure there are enough healthy, qualified canines to train as service animals for people in need, and to increase the United States' ability to feed and provide healthy nutritious meals to millions of starving people in America.

CPSIA information can be obtained at www.ICGtesting.com
Printed in the USA
BVOW03s1034221014

371882BV00011B/89/P